Piracy Today

Robbery and Violence at Sea since 1980

Bow and arrow men – a typical group of security guards hired locally to protect ships in the vicinity of West African ports.
Courtesy of Security Investigation Services, London.

PIRACY TODAY

Robbery and Violence at Sea since 1980

Captain Roger Villar

CONWAY
MARITIME PRESS

ISBN 0 85177 357 5

Design and maps drawn by Tony Garrett
Typesetting by Witwell Ltd, Liverpool
Printed and bound in the United Kingdom by The Thetford Press Ltd, Norfolk

Contents

Introduction

Piracy is as rife today as ever with over 400 armed attacks on shipping recorded as taking place in the brief period from 1980 to 1984. This record is undoubtedly the most comprehensive which exists, yet the information is still far from complete because of the great difficulties of uncovering the full story when nations, individuals and shipowners each have their own reasons for keeping the facts secret.

Some of these attacks demonstrate the gratuitous cruelty and inhumanity which characterised the old-time pirates; others are less bloody affairs involving attacks on ships in harbour. Pirates are invariably armed with knives such as the much favoured two-foot-long machete, but only occasionally with firearms. Nevertheless there have been occasions when pirates have used machine pistols and at least one incident when a ship has been completely taken over by raiders. Attacks occur world-wide from the Caribbean to the Indian Ocean, and the Far East. Although there have been comparatively few deaths other than in Far Eastern waters all types of attack can prove extremely frightening for the victims.

Many of these attacks do not constitute piracy within a precise legal sense as they have occurred within national territorial waters and should therefore strictly be defined as armed robbery. Nevertheless in this book the word piracy is used in its more widely understood meaning of armed attack at sea.

Very many authorities have been consulted in researching this book. I am grateful to all of them for their assistance and a list of acknowledgements follows on the next page. However, I am particularly grateful to Lieutenant Commander Miles Chapman who joined me to assist in the research and went on to contribute much to the whole book. Nothing would have been possible without his help.

Roger Villar

ACKNOWLEDGEMENTS

I am most grateful to the following, amongst many others, who have given their help in preparing and researching this book: the Hydrographer of the Navy; General Council of British Shipping; *Daily Telegraph*; *Bangkok Post*; Portsmouth Central Library; Department of Transport, Shipping Policy Division; *Fairplay Shipping Weekly*; International Cargo Crime Prevention; Mr Eric Ellen of the International Maritime Bureau; Lloyd's of London Press Ltd; *Dock and Harbour Authority Magazine*; *Shell World Magazine*; *Ports of the World Magazine*; *Dredging and Port Construction Monthly*; Port of Singapore Authority; US Coast Guard; US Department of Transport; United Nations High Commissioner for Refugees; International Red Cross; Captain E E Mitropoulos of the International Maritime Organisation; Mr Robert Stevens; the Nigerian Information Service; the Nigerian Port Authority; Norwegian Maritime Directorate; the Cruising Association of South Africa; Mr Don Street; Captain and Mrs John Hutchinson; Mr Peter Tangvald; *Yachting Monthly*; the Seven Seas Cruising Association; Republic of Singapore Yacht Club; Mr Tristan Jones; Captain H H Mcintosh; The Nautical Institute; Furness Withy Lines; Professor G Marston; BIMCO; West of England Ship Owners Insurance Services Ltd; Overseas Containers Ltd; International Shipping Federation; Mr Michael Mates MP; Merchant Navy and Airline Officer's Association; National Union of Seamen; *Seatrade Magazine*; Naval attachés and others of Brazil, Denmark, France, West Germany, Greece, the Netherlands, Norway, and Sweden; the Swedish Club (P&I); Pandibra (P&I Brazil); Danish Shipowners Association; Ministre d'Urbanisme, France; Der Bundesminster für Verkehr, West Germany; High Commissioner for Singapore; Swedish Shipowners Federation; Captain K L Row; Captain F le Messurier; Mr Richard Fleming; Mr M Athoe; Captain J B Jones; Captain R W Elenor; Nassau Shipyards Ltd; The New York Yacht Club; Mr Michael Burdick; Automar Shipping Line; Tsakos Shipping Line; Ocean Fleets Ltd; BP Shipping Ltd; Gotaas-Larsen Ltd; Buries-Marks (Ship Management) Ltd; Ping An Steamship (Hong Kong) Ltd; Dansk Esso Ltd; Nedlloyd Rederijdiensten BV; A F Harmstorf & Co; Mediterranean Shipping Co SA; Compagnie Navigation Denis Freres; Friomar Compania Naviera SA; Hugh Stinnes Zweigniederlassung Hamburg; Brostroms Rederi AB; Standard Shipping Co (Liberia); Compania Maritima del Nervion SA; Ben Line Steamers Ltd; Diamantis Pateros Ltd; Malaysian International Shipping Corporation BERHAD; Yawatahama Kisen Ltd; Mobil Shipping Co Ltd; CP Bulkships; Shell Tankers (UK) Ltd; Sanko Marine Co Ltd; Neptune Orient Line; Utah Transport Inc; Ceylon Shipping Corporation; Swedish Caledonian Marine Management Ltd; Regent Shipping Ltd (Hong Kong); Halfdan Ditlev-Simonsen & Co, Management A/S; Papachristidis Maritime Inc; Pallas Shipping Agency Ltd; World Wide Shipping Agency Ltd (Hong Kong); Chevron Shipping Co; Wheelock Marine Services Ltd.

PART I
PIRACY WORLD-WIDE

CHAPTER 1

Modern Piracy

A rmed attacks on merchant ships and yachts reached epidemic proportions in early 1981 with up to 12 ocean-going merchant ships being reported as under attack each day in the West African area alone. Raids have taken place in areas ranging from the Philippines and South China Sea to the Indian Ocean, West Africa, the Caribbean and South America. Although this book lists over 400 armed attacks as occurring between 1980 and 1984, unquestionably this forms only part of a world-wide story in which a large number of incidents remain unreported for a wide variety of reasons. Nor do these figures include the tragically cruel treatment of the Vietnamese boat people. Nearly half the 500 or so boats leaving Vietnam every year are attacked and refugees killed, women raped, and girls abducted. Piracy has developed in recent years into an increasingly organised and profitable business. Though its incidence waxes and wanes as trade patterns change, or as authorities take greater measures to control the trouble, there is little doubt that it will continue to grow.

There is however, almost nothing in today's piracy reminiscent of Captain Kidd or Captain Morgan or the many other old-time pirates who are now popularly seen as romantic heroes rather than cruel and bloody rogues. Those pirates looked for plunder on the high seas and were legitimate targets for any nation able to catch them. Few modern attacks are similar in nature apart from those taking place around the well-established pirate lairs in the Sulu Sea to the south of the Philippines, and in the Gulf of Siam where the well publicised attacks on the Vietnamese boat people have occurred. These demonstrate a casual cruelty and disregard for human life which defy description.

Most of today's incidents are of a quite different nature and occur when merchant ships are on passage in territorial waters or in harbour. It can be argued that such incidents do not constitute piracy according to the generally accepted law which evolved from past centuries by which piracy is held to be an act which occurs on the high seas. But that is itself highly debatable and, for the purposes of this book, piracy is defined as armed attack at sea. Much of it occurs where trading patterns bring considerable numbers of merchant ships into contact with the developing world where there are large numbers of people still living at low subsistence level – West Africa, Indonesia, and Brazil are classic examples. Where poverty is endemic, the sight of products from the rich Western world is an enormous temptation and almost anything can be of value – even polypropylene ropes which make excellent wigs in Nigeria!

The pattern in which this type of piracy develops is broadly similar everywhere. At first there may be extensive thieving from cargo and accommodation areas while ships are alongside and gangs of labourers are on board. It is all too easy to broach a few cases in the confusion of working cargo, or to slip away briefly from a working party to pry in the accommodation areas. Some gangs may be well organised and there is clear evidence from several areas, and West Africa in particular, that one or two members of a gang of labourers working cargo will steal away to survey the best areas for subsequent attack. In Nigeria, for example, there are cases where burnt paper torches have been found in the holds after cargo has been worked, indicating that someone has been snooping, and highlighting the danger should there be an inflammable cargo. If hatches are closed during heavy squalls in the rainy season, this merely gives an added opportunity for labouring gangs to leave their work to survey possible areas of attack.

Such relatively simple thieving is also sometimes the work of shore working parties and cases have occurred of ships' mooring ropes being cut, especially when they are of good quality nylon. The embarrassment to a ship moored in a 5–6 knot current is obvious.

However the first direct raids generally occur during the dark hours. A few young men will climb on board through the hawsepipe or up a grapnel and rope, steal whatever they can, and disappear as quickly as possible. Very occasionally they may have advance information from gangs of labourers of what to steal. In West Africa and off Singapore, they will often be barefoot wearing no more than a loin cloth and invariably carrying a two-foot-long machete which is an essential of daily life in a thickly vegetated and agricultural country. Even large merchant ships find it difficult with today's reduced crews to maintain more than two watchmen on deck and thus raiders find it easy to slip on board undetected in the dark.

Although driven to piracy by poverty and the temptation of

obviously wealthy merchant shipping, these robbers are not generally particularly brave or determined, and often retreat at the first sign of opposition. They steal whatever they can take quickly, looking for containers stowed on deck or open hatches. They may bring bolt-cutters able to deal with normal padlocks. Many have also quickly become familiar with the fact that the ship's safe is kept in the master's cabin, the key normally hidden in a desk drawer or the bookcase, and that the safe is seldom bolted down and can be taken away if it cannot be opened quickly. It is inevitable that the master's cabin should be a prime target and thus the master himself at risk.

However, as more money becomes available to finance attacks, robbery develops into an organised crime and attacks become more sophisticated operations. Bigger and more powerful craft may be used by attackers, such as the boats reported off Bangkok which can outrun police vessels, and the 25-knot speed of some of the craft used in Nigerian waters which sometimes work in large fleets. In December 1980 the 7550-ton *Nigerian Brewer* was attacked in Port Harcourt, Nigeria in full daylight by 12 large canoes powered by twin outboard motors and each containing five to six men.

These bigger craft make it viable for ships to be raided much further offshore – the 2741-ton *Snowfrost* was pirated 20 miles • Map p78-9 off the Benin coast in 1982 and the entire ship taken over by the raiders. They also enable ships to to be boarded while on passage at speeds of up to 13 knots or so, by approaching from astern and throwing up a grapnel and line. Such attacks are often reported in Indonesian waters off Singapore.

There is clear evidence, particularly from West Africa, that raiders sometimes have access to cargo manifests so that they know precisely which containers hold the most valuable and saleable loot. As gangs become more sophisticated they may amalgamate into major protection rackets which embrace even security guards hired by ships from the shore. The use of firearms may also become more general.

The nature of attacks varies from place to place. Sometimes they have a particularly violent character. The small Danish cargo ship *Lindinga Ivory* was attacked in 1979 when three miles off the Lagos fairway buoy, the master killed and thrown overboard and all 14 crew members wounded. However, on the whole there have been few casualties, despite occasional running battles, and use of the two-foot-long machete which remains a favourite weapon.

This type of piracy fluctuates according to circumstances such as changing trade patterns, and the steps taken by authorities to control crime. The worst area has been West Africa, particularly Nigeria, although a significant number of ships have been boarded while on passage in the area of the Singapore Straits. The incidence of raids fell off markedly in 1984 from a high point in late 1982 and early 1983 where an average of at least five ships a week were being attacked world wide. There is no valid explanation for this reduction which is as likely to be due, for example, to a recent falling off in Nigerian trade and declining number of ships in the area as it is to reported tighter control by shore authorities. The conditions and the poverty which gave rise to piracy still exist and there is every likelihood that the number of ships attacked will increase again. Meanwhile piracy is spreading to other areas such as Santos in Brazil, Bangkok in Thailand, and the Indian Ocean. This type of piracy is clearly becoming an established fact of life at sea.

Other types of piracy affect small coastal traffic and yachts rather than ocean-going merchantmen. There are well established pirate groups in the Sulu Sea and possibly in the Natunas Islands of the South China Sea, and drug smuggling gangs in the Caribbean. Terrorists have attacked a considerable number of boats in many different areas and there are also the numerous attacks on the Vietnamese boat people. All these types of attack are of an entirely different nature to those already discussed, and are often characterised by appalling cruelty and inhumanity. In August 1984 a small passenger vessel was attacked in the Sulu Sea with 33 people killed, 3 girls abducted and a total of 200,000 pesos (about £10,000) stolen. Acts of unimaginable violence occur – in the Gulf of Siam a young boy was hoisted up the mast by fish-hooks stuck through his thighs so that he could not avoid seeing his mother being raped. There is no sign of any decrease in this type of attack.

At present the world is not well organised enough to combat piracy and succeeds in stamping out only a few of these troubles. Indeed, in researching for this book it has not even been possible to find one authority which has a complete list of attacks which have taken place and which can thus state clearly what is happening and what action needs to be taken. Shipowners are often loath to give details of attacks on their ships lest they give offence to the country with which they are trading, or their insurance premiums are raised. Nations in whose waters piracy occurs are equally reluctant to discuss it, nor in the developing countries is it likely that they actually have the full details. Drug smuggling in the Caribbean for example is very much a closed book, though its general pattern is quite clear.

But if the world lacks factual information it does little about the problems of which it is aware. Defence of merchant shipping in territorial waters is left to the nation owning those waters and other nations do not intervene even though it can be argued that they have every right to do so. Attacks on merchant shipping largely occur in waters belonging to developing countries where the forces to control them effectively often do not exist. However, in Nigeria new security measures and patrols have helped to reduce piracy; a Thai anti-piracy programme to assist the Vietnamese boat people has been aided by funding from 11 nations. But such measures are minimal, for example some 50% of the Vietnamese refugee boats are still being attacked. Often such attacks are sighted by merchant ships which refuse to stop and help because of the ensuing delay and the difficulties of taking refugees to a foreign port.

Because official action has been negligible ships have become more and more responsible for their own defence and, despite the reduced crews (a result of economy measures), there are many steps which can be taken to make it more difficult for pirates to board, or to alert crews of a possible attack. Although many ships take basic precautions, such as remaining well offshore and without lights at night, few take steps which would cost a significant sum of money, simply because of their already marginal profits. Only the Soviets differ, though they refuse to be drawn onto the subject. It has been widely reported that a few years ago one of their merchant ships towed an empty small craft into Singapore harbour and reported that it had been found adrift. The inference was clear that the ship had made a completely successful and merciless defence against pirates, and it is thought that no Soviet ship has been attacked since. Equally yachtsmen who have been armed and ready have successfully defended themselves.

Pirates look, therefore, like continuing to have a relatively free hand in the future. The empires, fleets, and armed merchant ships which once contributed to their suppression have long since disappeared. As yet, despite some nasty incidents, little has occurred to disturb the world's conscience and force greater combative measures. The inhuman atrocities taking place in the Gulf of Siam have resulted only in the minimal funding of an anti-piracy programme; the attacks on ocean-going merchantmen have not led to serious inconvenience and loss of life and no effective measures have been initiated.

One cannot escape the feeling that the world does not want to know except when its pocket is touched. Since the demise of Pax Britannica, those who wish to survive must defend themselves.

CHAPTER 2

The West African Coast

The area considered here is the huge bulge on the west coast of Africa which extends from Dakar in the north to Douala in the south and includes the countries, Senegal, The Gambia, Guinea-Bissau, Guinea, Sierra Leone, Liberia, the Ivory Coast, Ghana, Togo, Benin, Nigeria, and Cameroun. Some 138 million people inhabit this area with 82 million of them in Nigeria. All suffer from the difficulties of developing nations and there are enormous differences in living standards and incomes between a few very rich and an immense number of very poor. The average production (derived by dividing the gross national product by the number of population) is no more than some $710 per head per year, compared with about $13,800 per head in America, nearly 19 times as great, and $8000 in Britain, over 11 times as great. Many people are engaged in little more than keeping themselves alive, often through agricultural pursuits, but agricultural management is poor and poverty is endemic. Populations are increasing and Nigeria's population of 82 million people has grown from only 55 million in 1963. The desert is slowly encroaching on the existing agricultural land to make poverty even worse. As a result populations migrate towards the coast where they hope to find more profitable work, though even there they find difficulty in obtaining a satisfactory living.

It is therefore natural that a proportion of the population has

• Map p78-9

turned to thievery merely to keep alive. Thieving has been endemic throughout this area for centuries; piracy is a natural development and there is no way, other than enforcing tough regulations and strict security, in which it can be controlled. It has been encouraged in recent years by an enormous expansion of trade, largely founded on Nigerian oil production, which began in the mid-1970s. Although this trade expanded throughout West Africa, in Nigeria up to 40 ships were queuing at any one time to enter Lagos, which was then incapable of handling such numbers. These vessels were obvious and easy targets. Pirates went for cargo rather than cash, breaking open containers to find whatever they could, and there was a ready market ashore for everything. Their prime targets were good quality cloth and fabrics, sophisticated electronics, pharmaceutical drugs which are in very short supply, and foodstuffs. There was no serious opposition from the authorities ashore.

The tactics used and the growth of piracy have been very much on the lines already described in the opening chapter. The main type of craft used has been the indigenous West African canoe hollowed out of a single tree trunk, with rough planking side boards to give greater freeboard and safety. Such canoes vary in length from 7–8 feet and carry a one-man crew ostensibly fishing and with a net to camouflage stolen cargo if stopped by the customs or police. They go up in size to large dug-out canoes capable of holding 8–12 people which again are ostensibly used for fishing although once they hold more than 3 or 4 people it is obvious that they have an ulterior motive. Some have been reported as being fitted with twin outboard motors giving them speeds of 25 knots, giving clear indication of the type of organisations financing them; no simple fisherman could afford such luxury.

The first attempts at piracy were generally spontaneous and haphazard in the manner already described but one or two incidents had more serious overtones. There are reports for the years 1975–1977 of a few ships in the Lagos Roads being attacked by gangs as large as 25 men and having their cargoes pillaged. The 726-ton *Idun* was attacked in 1977 while at anchor and her crew beaten-up and attacked with knives. The *Peter Star* was similarly attacked by about 25 pirates while at anchor and her cargo pillaged. The most frightening incident in these early years was that previously mentioned in chapter 1 in which the master of the *Lindinga Ivory* was shot and thrown overboard and the remainder of the crew wounded. On the whole little seems to have been done about such incidents by the authorities ashore, although the *Lindinga Ivory* case drew international attention and the Nigerian authorities ostensibly took drastic steps against those whom they believed responsible. As one ship's master reported 'Law and order are not strong points ...' The situation was to get much worse.

By 1980 trade was strong with many more merchant ships present and the frequency of incidents rose rapidly. It appears that at first these took the form of major pilfering, generally from ships working cargo alongside. In May of that year the master of a British ship at Apapa, Lagos, drew attention to the deplorable lack of security on the wharf where gangs of thieves were apparently openly roaming up and down waiting to loot cargo as soon as it was landed. A similar pattern appeared elsewhere on the West African coast, particularly in Sierra Leone and Ghana. At the same time however there were also a few reports of incidents showing a slightly greater degree of sophistication with thieves coming on board to throw cargo over the side into canoes which disappeared rapidly. Pirate craft began to follow ships into harbour and choose their moment to attack, since ships are particularly vulnerable whilst actually berthing alongside when the crew are fully occupied and shore-based security guards have not yet come on board.

Pirates began to concentrate more and more attention on ships waiting for berths, sometimes several miles out to sea. Gangs of up to 50 or so, frequently armed with knives and bottles and occasionally with guns, would roam as they pleased with little or no interference from the shore. A number of attacks, both offshore and alongside, appear to have been specifically based on information concerning a ship's cargo manifest, enabling the robbers to know where to go for the chief prizes. Some pirates even had the facility to jam VHF channel 16 on which ships would otherwise call for help.

Except on rare occasions assistance was not available from shore even when requested. Police actually on board ships have disappeared during an attack and police launches, known to be available, have failed to help ships under attack by a dozen or so large canoes. Although some ships hired native guards, like the 'bow and arrow' men, it seems likely that at least some of these were working in league with the pirates. Ships thus had virtually no outside assistance.

17

In December 1980 alone, 16 attacks are reported to have taken place in Nigerian waters compared with 4 for the rest of the West African coast. The 10,800-ton *Jonny Wesch* was boarded on five occasions in December 1980 while alongside the quay at Apapa and the crew were threatened with knives on at least one occasion. The French *Saint Jacques* was boarded in the same month in the early hours at Bonny by 75 men and the 6110-ton Dutch *Andrea Smits* a few days later by 40 to 50 men. Like all others, she too called repeatedly for assistance but none came. The pattern continued to be much the same for many months.

The story of the 6752-gross ton Panamanian vessel *Rafaela* is typical of many of that time. She anchored in Lagos Roads on 11 June 1981 and maintained a reinforced watch on deck because of the known threat of piracy. During the night she managed to repel numerous attempts at boarding over the bow and stern but the raiders threatened to come back and kill everybody on board. *Rafaela* moved out to anchor offshore for the night, returning to the roads in the morning. That day was peaceful and she remained in the roads overnight although a number of pirate boats approached her between 2200 and midnight. They were repelled by the whole crew who armed with sticks and iron bars succeeded in throwing off the hooks and grabs by which the pirates attempted to get on board.

By daybreak they felt more or less safe but there was still no berth available. It remained peaceful until about 2230 that night when *Rafaela* was 10½ miles off shore. Their radar showed several small boats about two miles away who could have been fishermen. But suddenly three large motor boats full of men came in at speed and attempted to board through the hawsepipe and by grapnel and line over the stern. *Rafaela* replied with her Very light pistols and distress rockets. The attackers were repelled and she got underway at full speed in an attempt to ram one attacking boat who opened fire on her before she moved further off shore. There was no reaction whatever from the shore authorities to her calls for help. Many of the crew were extremely shocked and nervous. Not unnaturally her owners agreed that she should divert elsewhere.

Shipowners were now beginning to voice strong complaints as were the European Economic Community (EEC), the International Shipping Federation, the International Transport Workers' Federation, as well as other organisations and national unions. There were fears of huge insurance claims and increased freight rates where threatened to offset possible losses. Seamen's organisations threatened a boycott of Lagos. In response to all this, in April 1981 Nigeria set up a ministerial task force to deal with the problem and two steps which resulted from this were the formation of a combined service harbour patrol force under the control of the navy, and the banning of outboard canoes from port areas. Furthermore Nigeria also promised to form a coast guard to maintain order in territorial waters.

There was an almost immediate effect. In the nine months from October 1981 to June 1982 there were only 6 attacks reported in Nigerian waters compared with 72 for the previous 9 months. But it didn't last. The frequency of attacks rose again in July 1982 with a total of 36 reported in the 9 months to March 1983. Pirates were now armed more frequently with hand guns, and on one occasion with machine guns. Just after Christmas Day 1982, the 12,007-ton Ro-Ro ship *Vegaland* moved 20 miles off from Lagos to avoid pirate attack and kept the main pumps going to provide a 'water barrier' defence system. But armed pirates were seen climbing on board shortly after 2300. At least three had hand guns and one a machine pistol and they soon had control of the bridge. The second mate was wounded in the leg and the motor man, the only crew member who had not succeeded in locking himself in the accommodation for safety, had to help the pirates carry stolen cargo to their canoes.

Nor was piracy entirely confined to Nigerian waters. The 2741-ton reefer *Snowfrost* was at anchor 16 miles off Benin in December 1982 and far enough out to think herself safe. Shortly after midnight, two large motor boats with some 15 Africans on board, came alongside unnoticed, seized a number of the crew, posted sentries at all the accommodation entrances, and then found their way to the master's cabin. He saw them coming and tried to close his cabin door in their faces until they shot at him. Thereafter they beat him until he showed them the ship's safe and then they had the run of the ship for three hours.

These two incidents alone illustrate the virtually complete control and freedom of action which these pirates have had. Recently there has been a quite dramatic reduction, with only six attacks having been reported in Nigerian waters since February 1983 and no more than one for the whole of 1984. Few details of these are available although it seems that pirates still operate in large gangs of 20 men or so armed with knives and bottles. Stronger measures introduced in Nigeria by the new military government which took control in December 1983 have unquestionably contributed to this reduction in attacks, to such an extent that the Director of the Nigerian Information Office was able to say in September 1984

The Nigerian government has taken a number of measures aimed at fighting sea piracy within her waters. Regular joint navy and customs patrols have paid off handsomely and as a result, the incidence of piracy generally has been on the decline for some time now. I am however unable to give statistics but it is safe to say that the measures which were intensified at the onset of the present military administration in the country have reduced the crime by more than ninety per cent.

In other West African countries, piracy has not been anywhere like as organised or on the same scale as in Nigeria though there have been a significant number of attacks reported – 30 in 1980, 18 in 1981, 5 in 1982, 14 in 1983 and 1 in 1984. A few have been affairs with armed pirates, such as the raid on the *Snowfrost* or the incident reported in 1984 when a gang of armed men stole equipment, spares and rope valued at $50,000 from the 16,499-ton bulk carrier *Akindynos C* at Freetown. At Matadi, Zaire, late in 1983 there were attacks on two ships by armed gangs who in one case had guns. Generally, however, raids have not been as organised as those in Nigerian waters and as a rule have involved the pilfering of cargo. In 1980 one ship reported that pilfering had reached epidemic proportions at Freetown, Sierra Leone; another said much the same about Tema, Ghana. In 1981 neither police nor customs officers could prevent excessive pilferage of cargo from the 12,335-ton *Nedlloyd Fresco* at Dakar and the same pattern is apparent at Monrovia, Liberia, and so on throughout the West African coast. Once again, however, there has been a dramatic fall in the incidence of such raids with only one reported for the whole of 1984.

Does that dramatic fall to only two raids during the whole of 1984 mean that piracy in this area is declining and if so what has caused this decline? To deduce this the factors which have given rise to piracy must be examined. There is, firstly, no sign of any significant alleviation of poverty along the West African coast – a problem which is tending to worsen. People will continue to migrate to the coast, they will be forced to steal, and they will find a ready market for virtually any type of loot.

Secondly, corruption is so rife in many West African countries that the normal forces of law and order familiar in the West do not exist. In part this is because lack of money prevents the police from having the advantages of modern equipment and facilities which are taken for granted in the developed world. Finger printing equipment is, for example, generally impossible to get hold of; even basic photography may be a problem. All of the state services operate under handicaps which are unknown elsewhere and they have little hope of becoming efficient. But the roots of the problem are deeper than this - ships have called for help on innumerable occasions without result, policemen have turned their backs on thieving even when they can actually see it taking place; inefficiency and venality are rife. Even when arrests are made, those responsible for implementing the law (both police and judiciary) may have a vested interest in the cases being considered. Recruitment to such posts is not made by selection procedures based on merit common to more developed countries, but by nepotism, tribal allegiance, or for political reward, and much the same system may govern promotion. Cases exist of police officers of superintendent rank who have been completely illiterate with a correspondingly slight grasp of the technicalities of the law. Bribery is widespread. Large groups of criminals may terrorise their own districts and attack anyone who gives evidence, or takes action against them. When all these factors combine with endemic poverty, there is a great opportunity for adventurous men to take advantage of relatively easy pickings and to sell their goods easily.

Thirdly, are the opportunities which exist for piracy and robbery. All merchant ships have relatively small crews and are strongly encouraged, with the possible exception of the Soviets, to be unarmed. Although a number employ native 'bow and arrow' men to deter intruders, there is a strong suspicion that some of these are part of the same protection rackets which support the pirates. Nor is there any record of even one arrow having found its mark. Pirates and thieves can therefore generally gain easy access to ships and meet with little opposition unless assistance is given from the shore.

The conditions which give rise to piracy thus clearly exist in many countries. The frequency and extent of raids, however, obviously correlate closely to the amount of ships present, and this number has fluctuated widely as trade with West Africa has grown or declined. With the increased trade pattern of the 1970s and early 1980s (already referred to in Nigeria), and the low capacity of the ports, large numbers of ships had to lie off shore and so formed easy targets. The number of attacks on ships increased in consequence, and, with growing experience, the pirates' methods have become more sophisticated. The recent apparent reduction in piracy in Nigeria may have resulted from the decline in trade caused by the fall in the market for oil, and a shrinking Nigerian economy. In addition the port of Lagos has been improved and ships no longer have to wait so long for a berth. Nigeria is also taking strong action to stamp out crime and corruption.

There is no evidence that such strong steps are being taken in other West African countries. It therefore seems illogical that they too should have seen the same dramatic fall in the incidence of attacks. That points clearly to the most significant factor being the reduction in trade which has reduced the number of targets rather than new security measures.

Piracy is therefore likely to continue to be a potential threat for a very long time. The same factors are likely to contribute to its continuance – endemic poverty, lax security, and corruption. Nor are significant steps being taken to enable merchantmen to guard themselves. If trade increases again, we may expect something of a repetition of past events, though perhaps not on the scale where reports have been given of up to 12 ocean-going merchant men being attacked daily in just one major port.

CHAPTER 3

The Singapore Area

Singapore and the Strait of Malacca offer enormous opportunities for pirates, having the heaviest concentration of merchant shipping anywhere in the world. One merchant ship arrives or departs at Singapore roughly every twelve minutes, night and day, throughout the year and 200 ships a day pass through the Strait of Malacca. It is an obvious feasting ground for pirates and, while their attacks have never reached the epidemic proportions of West Africa, over 150 incidents have been reported for 1981–1984. The character of the attacks, and the underlying reasons for them, have however been substantially different to those occurring in West African waters and the majority have been made on ships underway, rather than those in harbour or awaiting a berth.

The Strait of Malacca is the main passage for all shipping between East and West. It is shaped like a funnel and is quite wide at its western end but starts to narrow some 200 miles north-west of Singapore, and continues to narrow until it is barely more than a mile wide immediately south of Singapore itself. Because of the narrowness of the Strait and the mass of shipping using it, separation zones have been created immediately south of Singapore. Eastbound shipping uses the southernmost Phillip Channel and westbound shipping passes • Map p80-1 close to the north. Generally shipping will transit at speeds of up to about 13 knots. Many ships also anchor off Singapore whilst awaiting a berth in the harbour.

There are thus many tremendously attractive targets for pirates within both Singaporean and Indonesian territorial waters. It is almost a pirates' dream opportunity – all they require is a suitable base, some means of getting on board ships underway or at anchor, and a market for their loot.

Singapore does not welcome pirates and controls their activities successfully. Her population of some 2½ million are crowded onto a small main island of 224 square miles and 54 smaller off-lying islands, and have the highest standard of living of any nation in the Far East with the exception of Japan. They live by seaborne trade, have every intention of defending their right to trade peacefully and, though their defence forces are small, they are efficient.

The situation is unfortunately very different on the south side of the main channel only a few miles away. Indonesia has a totally different make-up and character with far greater opportunities open for young fit men who wish to break the law. She is much larger than Singapore, stretches 3200 miles from east to west, has some 3000 small offshore islands, lies across three time zones and has a population of 158 million. But she is very poor with an average annual production of no more than $460 per head – even less than in West Africa. Many people live at or below subsistence level and the defence forces are small with largely old equipment, and little hope of exercising tight control over such an extensive coast line.

With so much rich merchant shipping on their doorstep there is every temptation for young Indonesian men to become pirates. It is thought there are a number of pirate bases along the length of the Malacca Strait since ships have been attacked over a quite widespread area. However, the chief base is clearly in the Riau Islands immediately south of Singapore situated on the southern edge of the channel at almost its narrowest point. These islands are densely vegetated with many narrow passages and coral reefs which make them excellent hiding places, and their indigenous population of fishermen offers splendid and natural cover. Pirates based there thus operate in relative seclusion and have little difficulty in reaching shipping on passage, or in getting to the Singapore anchorages only a few miles further north. Their opportunities are increased further by the modern practice in which ships avoid entering Singapore harbour to take on stores because of the cost of the harbour dues, and instead resupply while steaming at slow speed, from launches sent out from Singapore.

Many attacks have been on ships in passage in the eastbound Phillip Channel where masters have to concentrate intensely on safe navigation in narrow waters requiring a number of course changes. Pirates do not operate in the large co-ordinated groups found elsewhere, but generally in small groups of two to five men, although some reports of larger parties of up to ten have been received. Those that have been seen are typically dark skinned and barefoot, wearing a loin cloth, and a bandana tied round the head. Invariably they are armed with at least a machete or knife but as yet not with firearms. They run up to the targeted ship in a fast outboard prahu (native skiff) some eight to ten feet long, approach from astern to avoid forward looking radar and look-outs, and use grappling hooks to reach the deck. Once there they will cut a length off a convenient mooring rope to be lowered over the stern for a quick get-away. In the right conditions they have been known to carry out a raid completely unseen, or to get away together with their loot within six minutes of first being detected. Sometimes they hold up the crew with knives or machetes but a majority clearly prefer to remain unseen. The chief navigational dangers arise when pirates succeed in holding a crew at knife-point. Such an attack was made on the 29,960-ton tanker *Corsicana* in August 1981 while the bridge team were navigating through the narrow eastbound Phillip Channel at night at 12 knots. Three pirates were suddenly seen climbing up the bridge ladder. They put machetes and knives at the throats of the second officer and helmsman while they forced the master to go to his cabin to open his safe. While the master was thus forced below, the second officer made a course alteration even though the pirate standing over him ordered him not to. The raiders had gone within six minutes of being seen and cut the bridge telephone lines as they left. By the time the upper deck lighting could be switched on, they had disappeared.

There were 21 raids of this nature on ships in the Phillip Channel in 1981 beginning with the introduction of the new traffic separation scheme in May; a further 19 in 1982, and 11 in 1983. On no occasion do the pirates appear to have been spotted until they appeared on deck. Quite often, as with the raid on the 40,000-ton tanker *Mammoth Monarch* in September 1981, the raid is only discovered when the master leaves the bridge momentarily to go below and finds his cabin ransacked, the safe gone, and a length of rope (cut from a convenient reel) hung over the stern. Raids are invariably carried out at night and no pirates have yet been venturesome enough to attempt one in broad daylight. Ships are now advised to avoid night transits of the Channel.

So it has continued until very recently. In July 1983 the 41,256-ton liquified petroleum gas carrier *Stena Oceanica* was passing through the Phillip Channel at night at 13 knots. The crew had every reason to believe they were safe; no pirates were seen. But shortly before midnight the chief officer found that the master's cabin had been ransacked and the ship's safe taken. The radio officer was found tied up on the poop deck after having surprised five men and been held at knife-point. In all, the pirates were on board for 30 minutes without being noticed.

Attacks are of much the same character in the more northerly westbound channel. In March 1983, the 129,882-ton bulk carrier *Orco Trader* had just left Singapore and was heading south-west for Raffles Light before turning to the west. They were prepared for attack and had instructed the crew that, should this occur, the engine room personnel should remain isolated in the engine room, the radio officer in the radio room, and the crew lock themselves in their cabins. The watch on the bridge maintained constant vigil using radar to give as much warning as possible of approaching craft but this proved virtually useless because the mass of small craft present in the area made it impossible to distinguish potential pirates.

At 2330, when three miles from Raffles Light, the master left the bridge briefly to go to his cabin. As he arrived there he met six dark-complexioned young men wearing dark T-shirts and shorts and some barefooted. All were carrying large knives and were coming towards the bridge. They grabbed him by the armpit and face and forced him to the deck holding a knife in his face and in his side. Repeatedly they said 'Shut up, money, money, money!' In the struggle he received a five-inch cut on one side of his nose which bled profusely, and his shirt was stained red by the blood. Clearly the pirates had not expected a struggle and in the confusion he managed to push them aside and ran for the bridge while they chased after him. Once there he shut the wheelhouse door and raised the alarm, alerted Singapore Marine Police on VHF radio, and turned on all the deck lights. Nothing more was seen of the pirates apart from 14 metres of six-inch hawser which had been cut off and trailed over the stern to form an escape route.

Pirates are having less success in the Singapore anchorages because of the steps taken by the Singapore authorities to combat their activities. Nevertheless their bases are thought to be within easy reach of the Singapore anchorages which stretch for about nine miles from Jurong in the west to east of Singapore harbour. This area forms a vast complex of wharves, oil terminals and anchorages, and Singapore's defence forces, efficient though they are, are not large enough to completely prevent attacks on shipping so exposed.

The first available report of raids on ships at anchor in the Singapore area came in August 1980 when the 89,730-ton *Hellespont Pride* was raided in the west anchorage. It was no more than a case of simple robbery, though the two intruders were armed with long knives and threatened the master and third officer and tied their hands.

Thereafter there were some months of apparent peace in the anchorages until March 1981. In that year the Singapore authorities reported seven ships as having been raided within their territorial waters. This figure rose to 13 in 1982 and dropped to 8 in 1983 and has continued to follow a similar pattern.

In the early hours of 17 September 1981 Captain Jones arrived by air from England with a relief crew to take charge of the 30,000-ton tanker *Fort Coulonge* in the Western Anchorage off Jurong. At just after 0400, the weather in Singapore was much as usual – warm with a light rain and not much wind. Captain Jones was sleeping deeply following his journey and his suitcase was still locked and packed beside his bunk. The door to his cabin was hooked back to allow some air to give him relief from the heat and humidity.

Suddenly the light went on. Three young Asians stood over him, each armed with a two-foot-long knife. Swiftly they tied his hands together with raffia (which they had brought with them) and all the time they kept up a chant 'Keep quiet – where is your money?'. The shock was immense. With a knife pricking his throat, Captain Jones had little option but to show them his wallet and cash. They then demanded the key to the ship's safe which was in his cabin. Uncomfortably aware that he had just drawn $80,000 to pay off the old crew, Captain Jones insisted that he did not have the key. But they went on and on – 'Where are the keys, where are the keys?' Meanwhile they ransacked the cabin: the desk, the drawers, everything. They dragged him over to the safe and went on with their questioning while he explained as convincingly as he could that he had only just come on board and the chief steward still had the keys ready to turn the cash over to him in the morning. He pointed to the still packed suitcase as confirmation.

At last it appeared that the robbers believed him and he was thrown on his bunk, his feet tied, and a blanket flung over his head. There was silence for what seemed an eternity while he wondered whether one of the long knives was going to descend on him. Finally he heard the outer door open, pushed off the blanket, and found himself alone. Struggling to the phone, he alerted the cadet on watch who sounded the alarm and freed him. He could see no sign of the raiders. The donkeyman, alerted by the alarm, had seen three young men climbing over the stern and picked up an iron bar as the only available weapon, but thought it unwise to fight against such odds. The robbers slipped into a fast boat and disappeared in a southerly direction. The raid had taken no more than ten minutes from start to finish though, to Captain Jones, it seemed an eternity.

All these attacks were relatively simple and none of them resulted in death or even serious injury. The pirates clearly rely on surprise tactics. They greatly prefer to operate unseen and are after cash, which is more portable than cargo. The master is therefore a prime target since the safe is normally kept in his cabin. On at least one occasion, a ship underway off Singapore, taking in stores from a shore launch (to avoid the necessity of entering harbour), has been boarded by pirates taking advantage of the bustle and confusion and the safe removed without anyone noticing – a profit of $50,000 is not a bad day's wage between four men. Ships with low freeboard such as tankers tend to be the main targets since they are easier to board from a small boat whilst underway.

Since reports of piracy began to come in, the Singapore authorities have stepped up their patrols in territorial waters, particularly at night. The authorities concerned, (the Marine Department and the Port of Singapore Authority under the Ministry of Communications, the Navy, the Ministry of Defence, and the Marine Police), now act in concert. They have a special VHF radio frequency for reporting incidents and they advise ships on the measures to be taken to prevent unauthorised boarding and recommend that transits of the Straits should not be undertaken in darkness. They nevertheless remain extremely reluctant to intervene in the Indonesian territorial waters of the Phillip Channel and have even requested Interpol's assistance.

By contrast the other areas of Indonesia which abut the Straits are not commercially important and the Indonesians neither feel the same compulsion to safeguard their waters nor can they afford to do so. The country simply does not have the resources to patrol the whole of its extensive coastline and tens of thousands of off-lying islands. Indonesia did step up her patrols, both by boat and helicopter, in early 1982, but the effect has been minimal. Pirates continue to live in the Riau Islands, and, if they are ever embarrassed by hot pursuit, they have little difficulty in slipping from the territorial waters of one state to those of another barely six miles away. Piracy here is not yet considered as a matter for international action because, (as will be seen in chapter 9) it does not constitute true piracy which has been defined by the United Nations as a 'crime committed on the high seas outside the jurisdiction of any state' where every nation has the duty to go to the aid of a ship under attack. Legally these raids are no more than armed robbery and it is the responsibility of either Singapore or Indonesia to deal with them as appropriate.

Surprisingly perhaps, piracy appears to have decreased from 48 attacks in 1983 to a mere 8 or so in 1984. This may not be the final figure because it takes time for reports to come in, and the official figures for the second half of 1984 have not been published yet. There does appear to be some seasonal trend in the frequency of attacks with the greatest number occurring from July to December and, if this is so for 1984, then the final figure will be larger. Equally it may be that new steps, such as the Singapore authorities' advice to transit only by day, are at last beginning to have an effect. Certainly there is no evidence that the Indonesians are taking any firmer steps than before to deal with their pirates or to flush out their lairs other than one report of a group of pirates being arrested early in 1985.

The unique feature about these attacks is that they are made largely against ships which are underway. Therein lies the main danger – that one day the crew of a major ocean-going merchantman will be forced into making a navigational error in a crowded and narrow channel. Should this occur to a laden monster tanker, the ecological consequences of a collision or grounding in these waters would be disasterous as in this area fishing is one of the main industries and fish a staple food. The *Corsicana*, as we have seen, came close to this situation. Who can say what may occur in the future, when the safe navigation of a ship may depend on the whims of an uneducated young man wielding a machete.

CHAPTER 4

East of Singapore

During the first half of the nineteenth century, the waters round China and Hong Kong were infested with pirates. At one time a woman commanded a fleet of 800 large junks and 70,000 men. They were eventually eliminated by the British fleet towards the middle of the century, who then turned their attention to combating pirates elsewhere throughout the Far East, including the Dyaks in Borneo. All of these pirate gangs were exceptionally cruel and some of their practices are revealed in *Pirates* by David Mitchell, (Thames and Hudson, 1976). Captured crews were given the chance of joining the Chinese pirates or dying very painfully. Unfortunate crew members were hoisted up the mast by their hands tied behind their backs, flogged, hoisted higher and given an hour to contemplate, then lowered to see if they had changed their minds. This process was repeated until they agreed to join the gang or died. The attitude to women is revealed by the Chinese pirates' law that 'no person shall debauch at his pleasure captured women; he shall first ask the quartermaster for permission and then go aside in the hold.'

These old time pirates are long extinct though they appear to have passed their customs on to their successors in the Gulf of Siam and the Philippines area. Pirates in other parts of the world are but kindly amateurs compared with these characters who have an almost universal and total disregard for human life and display a casual cruelty which surpasses anything found elsewhere. Both the Vietnamese boat people and innocent travellers have been, and continue to be, the victims. Where else could such horrifying incidents as those mentioned in chapter 1 have occurred, or of men and women being herded on to a small island so that they could be hunted, and the women raped. The inhumanity of such acts at least equals anything seen in past history.

All the evidence available verifies that these attacks and those recounted in Part III are true stories. Although piracy is a secretive business, the distances east of Singapore vast, and communications poor, sufficient information is becoming available to construct a broad and sound picture of piracy in the 1500 square mile area between Singapore, Taiwan, and Java. No reports have been received of incidents north of Taiwan and along the Chinese mainland where the large Chinese navy doubtless keeps pirates in control, nor of any attacks in the far flung waters of the Pacific.

Generally ocean-going merchantmen are not targets to the east of Singapore since a majority pass far from land down the centre of the South China sea. Nevertheless for those that do approach land the dangers can be very real. The 24,037-ton *Oriental Ambassador* was boarded by the 'Morning Glory' gang while sheltering in Manila Bay in the Philippines in May 1980. The gang appear to have after money in common with the other attacks discussed so far, but they were armed with automatic weapons and held up the master in his cabin. He was killed by a burst from an Armalite rifle while apparently trying to push a revolver away from his neck, and a Hong Kong engineer was wounded. It was particularly tragic that Captain Dyason, a much respected man, was on his last voyage before retirement when this took place.

• Map p82–3

However, this incident is probably unique to the Philippines for recent years, moreover five of the eight-strong gang were later caught. At the time of this attack the Philippine coast guard was making a concerted effort to break up gangs have which had been preying sporadically on foreign shipping in the anchorage off Manila Bay south harbour, and off Lamao and

Bataa. Since then, these gangs have turned to attacking local fishing, passenger, and cargo boats in Manila Bay instead.

In these waters east of Singapore one sees the same pattern of attacks on ocean-going merchant ships as elsewhere in the world. Merchant ships leaving Bangkok find themselves attacked in the vicinity of the pilot station by 15 to 20 pirates. They use fast 20-metre boats which resemble police craft but which can attain speeds of 30–40 knots enabling them to outpace the opposition. It is thought that in most instances these pirates know precisely which container holds the cargo they are seeking. This seems to be a relatively new sophisticated and organised development which will doubtless grow.

There have otherwise only been sporadic reports of piracy of ocean-going merchantmen. The 256,632-ton tanker *World Unicorn*, at anchor off Jakarta as a storage vessel, was raided in the early hours of February 1982 by two Indonesians who tied up the quartermaster and then forced the master at knife-point to open his safe. In September 1984 the 37,009-ton tanker *Santo Trader* was robbed one evening while alongside at Cilacap in Java. Two men armed with large machetes entered the master's cabin and forced him to open the safe before leaving him bound and gagged. Such incidents are very similar to those occurring in many other areas. They have not yet reached a level at which they could be of serious concern to the shipping community.

However, there is cause for concern in areas where known nests of pirates exist and these are: the Natunas Islands and Spratly Island which lie in the South China Sea in the centre of this wide passageway between East and West; the Sulu Sea which lies between Borneo and the Philippines; and, of course, the Gulf of Siam between Cambodia and Thailand.

The Natunas and Spratly Island
Reports from this area are sufficient to show that pirates are active but not in any great strength. The 7998-ton *Rio Colorado* is reported to have been attacked off Sabah in 1978 but no details of her position nor the incident are available. In early 1982 the Malaysian fishing boat *Ikan Mas* was working off the Natunas Islands when she saw a craft approaching which at first was identified as a Malaysian police boat. As it drew nearer, it could be seen to be full of men armed with sub-machine guns and was actually flying the skull and cross-

bones. Though no-one was killed or wounded, the pirates stole £40,000 worth of cash, fish and valuables. In April 1983 the yacht *Sidharta* was shelled and set on fire off Spratly Island and one crew member killed but it has been suggested that this was the work of Vietnamese soldiers rather than pirates. Six months later the Saudi Arabian *Sara Hashim* was attacked in the same area. Generally though, the waters to the north-west of Brunei and Sarawak appear to be well under control, and the menace further offshore in Malaysian waters has not been severe.

The Philippines and the Sulu Sea

The Philippines form a mass of separate islands stretching some 750 miles from north to south and 300 miles from east to west. Opportunities for piracy abound everywhere and it is clearly prevalent.

The area which is of most concern lies in the waters dividing the Sulu and Celebes seas between Borneo and the Philippine's southernmost island of Mindanao. This 200-mile wide gap is full of small islands and shoals of which the most notorious appears to be the Tawitawi group. It is obvious that a number of pirate groups exist here and elsewhere. In 1979 Peter Tangvald's wife was killed when pirates boarded his yacht, and in the same year a ferry was also taken over and three passengers killed. In July 1981 the *Iliana Bay* was hijacked off Mindanao and forced to proceed to another destination to unload her cargo of rice. The master was killed and several passengers wounded when they refused to help with the unloading. A month later the small 135-ton ferry *Nuria 767* was taken-over by two stowaways and two crew members, who lined up and shot 11 people; 48 others jumped overboard, of whom 25 drowned. As recently as August 1984 a small motorised launch crossing from Semporna to the Philippines was attacked by three men armed with sub-machine guns, and 33 of the 51 people on board were killed, including all the men and ten of the women. Others were wounded, and three young girls were abducted.

There have been other attacks on ships around the Philippines, the most recent in January 1985 when four 'locals' tried to board the cruise liner *Coral Princess* as she entered Cebu harbour at dawn in January 1985.

The most serious attacks have been in this area and the majority of pirates appear to operate at the most western end of the gap, displaying a total disregard for life in pursuit of their own gain.

The Gulf of Siam

The most repellent acts of piracy occur in the Gulf of Siam. Both Vietnamese boat people and Thai fishermen are the victims. This Gulf is bordered on the east by Vietnam and Cambodia and on the west by Thailand, and its maximum width is some 300 miles. Within it are around 27,000 registered Thai fishing boats and probably as many again which are not registered. A majority of the people in this area are poor, the average wage of a crew man being no more than 1100 baht a month (£34). This is a good income compared to standards elsewhere in Thailand. Existence is a struggle, and regard for life not great. The fishermen are themselves often part-time pirates and responsible for the majority of the attacks. But there are others who prey on the fishermen too, as well as on other more helpless victims. In December 1981 a trawler returning from Burma was attacked. All nine crewmen were shot dead and their belongings taken by men armed with M16 rifles. In January 1982, five Thais were arrested for having pirated and stolen two Malaysian trawlers. In April a gang of nine attacked a small fishing boat off An Thong island. As reported in chapter 6, one yachtsman off Songkla almost became the victim of a protection racket when he was surprised by a large grey boat coming alongside at night with men on deck armed with carbines, ready to jump on board.

But whatever some of these fishermen may suffer themselves, it is in dealing with Vietnamese boat people that they show the other side of their characters. Even by local standards, they act with unbelievable ferocity. Every woman is a target for rape, any resistance or action interpreted as aggravation is met by death, young girls are frequently abducted and are passed from boat to boat on a continual round of rape. There are cases where they have been bartered in exchange for goods, even fish. There can be little doubt that the fishermen in the Gulf of Siam are largely responsible for these attacks, and they follow a distinct pattern.

A majority of refugees come by boat round the southern corner of Vietnam and head straight for the southern part of Thailand barely 300 miles away. They are crammed into small boats with all their worldly possessions, which have often been converted into easily portable valuables, such as gold.

Such a large number of craft have already left Vietnam that refugees sailing today can often only do so in boats which are unseaworthy. In May 1979 it was reported that over 2000 refugees were escaping by boat each month; over 24,000 a year. Agreements were made with Hanoi to limit the numbers and they fell, from 15,598 in 1981 to 5913 in 1982 and 3383 in 1983. Yet even in the 12 months from May 1982 to April 1983, 463 refugee boats landed in Thailand and Malaysia.

At first, some 80% of these craft were attacked by pirates. The percentage had fallen to 47% for the first half of 1984 and the situation remains much the same today. Many refugees encounter merchant ships but most of these turn a blind eye rather than be troubled with the problems and possible delay involved in landing them at their next port of call, even though the procedure for doing so is now well established. The first attacks are usually by Thai fishing vessels shortly after the refugee craft rounds the tip of Vietnam and enters the Gulf of Siam. But pirates must take care not to attack too soon since Vietnamese military patrol boats operate in this area and have attacked Thai fishing vessels as well as refugees. This first set of attackers will, quite simply, come alongside and steal any valuables which they can find. There is a clear priority to be the first to rob the boat because usually there will very shortly be a second attack during which the boat will be stripped of everything which remains. Then will come a third, or a fourth, when the attackers will take revenge for not finding anything valuable to steal. They may ram the refugee boat until it sinks and abduct as many of the women as they want, or lie alongside for a considerable time while the women are taken on board and raped for up to 17 hours. Any men who resist will be clubbed to death, and all will eventually be left to drown except for the girls whom they abduct to be passed from hand to hand through the fishing fleet. It is reported that between 1980 and the end of 1983, 1376 Vietnamese boat people had been killed by pirates, 2283 women raped, and 592 women abducted. The United Nations High Commission for Refugees calculates that, on average, each refugee boat is attacked 3.5 times during its crossing.

Reports show very clearly what has been happening to those who have been captured and the girls and women who have been abducted. In late 1979 three refugee boats with 191 refugees on board were spotted by four pirate boats. The refugee boats were boarded by 50 pirates who beat up the men with clubs. The survivors were taken to the island of Koh Kra off the coast of southern Thailand and set free. It is a small island which must have appeared a haven of lush jungle, beaches and warm sea to the survivors. But word spread throughout the pirate community of their presence and dozens began to hunt down and attack the survivors, raping the women. One woman hid in the long grass but was burnt out by pirates who soaked it in gasoline; a man with three gold teeth had them removed first by smashing them with a rifle butt and then with pliers. At one point in this ordeal which lasted months, 47 pirate boats were encountered in Koh Kra's inlet.

Over 160 people are believed to have died on Koh Kra in the summer of 1979 alone. During the same period, 1250 persons were rescued from the island by the United Nations High Commission for Refugees which hired fishing trawlers and now has its own boat for the purpose. When the refugees departed they left notices – 'First you will be given something to eat; then everything will be taken away from you, even your clothes. They will rape you, boatload after boatload; they will come in their hundreds and rape you in turn. Then they will kill you.'

As for the girls abducted – in October 1981 a naval boat on routine patrol along the Songkhla coast investigated a trawler. Hearing a scream from below, they found a 15-year-old Vietnamese girl being raped by the skipper. She said that she and 41 others had escaped from Vietnam one year earlier and had been attacked three times. When there were no valuables left, the pirates took turns to rape the five girls on board and then abducted them. They were then passed from trawler to trawler and the 15-year-old had been given to two fishing trawler crewmen.

In November 1983, at Pulau Redang off the north-eastern Malaysian state of Trengganu, two Vietnamese women jumped off a Thai trawler and swam ashore to safety. More than 100 Thai fishermen in 18 trawlers approached the island to demand the return of the women. When a Malaysian naval boat approached, the blockade of trawlers prevented it from coming in until warning shots were fired.

It is possible to continue with an interminable account of cruelty and death. Many have been shocked by the tragic reports and as a result private rescue boats have been funded, such as the West German 5300-ton *Cap Anamur* which has to date rescued over 9000 refugees. An anti-piracy programme was set up in February 1981, initially with USA financial assistance, largely based on helping the Royal Thai Navy to defend its own waters. Then the United Nations High Commission for Refugees took over eight months later with donations from Australia, Canada, Denmark, Germany, France, Italy, Japan, the Netherlands, Norway, Switzerland, the United Kingdom, and the USA, initially totalling £3.6 million. But the task is immense with huge areas to control and thousands of fishing boats to monitor. The anti-piracy unit consists of no more than three 16-metre fast patrol craft, about 5 surveillance aircraft, 3 special operation task trawlers, and roughly 130 naval personnel. Even twice that force would have little chance of covering so large an area effectively.

Nor is it easy to find the aggressors. There are approximately 55,000 fishing craft in the Gulf of Siam. The registered craft are only distinguishable from the unregistered by a number on the side of the vessel consisting of a provincial indicator in Thai script followed by Arabic numerals. Even if a victim can recall the numerals, he has little chance of remembering the Thai script. Boat registration takes place in each province and there are no central records.

Nevertheless the anti-piracy programme and the action of private organisations appear to be having an effect, with a reported reduction of 20% in the incidence of attacks – a figure of 90% would perhaps be more significant. These statistics are based on the testimony of survivors and it can be assumed that many more die and incidents thus remain unrecorded. If progress is being made, it is extremely slow and uncertain. The suffering and the deaths continue.

CHAPTER 5

Central and South America

C entral and South America are the traditional home of revolution, and the Caribbean of buccaneering and piracy. Four hundred years ago the buccaneers in Hispaniola set the pattern for many of today's raids. They attacked Spanish shipping in dug-out canoes packed with marksmen, kept their bows towards their victim so as to present the narrowest possible target while they moved in close, and then after jamming the rudder swarmed up the stern. Similar attacks take place today both in South American waters and other parts of the world. In the Caribbean however, the main threat is to yachtsmen and small craft rather than ocean-going merchantmen; this is covered more fully in chapter 6.

The standard of living in a country generally correlates to the extent of piracy and robbery. Taking the average national annual production per head in Britain of US $8000 as a guide, and as producing a standard of living which does not encourage the need for piracy, the equivalent average figures for Brazil, Colombia, and Ecuador lie between US $1350 and US $1730 and there are enormous inequalities of wealth between the rich and poor. Correspondingly crime begins to proliferate as poor people seek to maintain an adequate standard of living by any means – not to the extent with which this occurs in West Africa where the equivalent average annual production figures are even lower but nevertheless to a significant extent. Somewhat similarly the Central American countries of Nicaragua, Guatemala, El Salvador and Honduras have even lower average annual production figures per head of between $670 and $1100 which correlates to the troubles • Map p86-7 which are occurring in these countries. In contrast, no serious piratical attacks have been reported from Venezuela where the oil industry gives an average annual production of about $4350 per head, which is clearly sufficient to make armed robbery and piracy much less prevalant.

SOUTH AMERICA
Colombia and Ecuador
Colombia and Ecuador appear to have a worse reputation for piracy than they deserve. Both are theoretically good breeding grounds for piracy and lawlessness having low living-standards, and expanding trade bringing more merchant shipping to the area. Colombia has an 1800-mile coastline almost equally divided between the Caribbean and Pacific coasts. Piracy has been a prolific source of trouble, but the number of attacks on ocean-going merchant ships which occurred only a few years ago appears possibly to have been brought under control, though a danger to yachts and small craft remains. The country is large and sparsely populated with 28 million people (mostly mestizos) spread over nearly half a million square miles. Much of the population is concentrated on the coastline with large empty spaces in the

forests of the interior. The economy is poor and largely agricultural with many small holdings and much production of coffee. Communications are difficult because of the mountainous nature of the country where the bulk of the population live at altitudes of between 4000 and 9000 feet. There are few roads and railways and their construction is difficult; even telephones are few with no more than some 1.8 million in service in 1982 and 37% of those concentrated in the capital of Bogota.

The political climate is volatile. There are left wing guerillas as well as right wing groups and the army is active in politics. Drug production and smuggling are rife. Both marijuana and the coca-tree (the basis for cocaine) grow naturally and whole villages and families may be dependent on them for their livelihood. Wrecking, by placing false lights and leading marks, has been practised on much the same lines as it used to be by the wreckers on the Cornish coast. White slavery is a profitable sideline. Almost inevitably there is widespread envy of the richer Western world whose wealth is manifested in its merchant shipping. Colombian trade has been expanding with the total of imports and exports with the United Kingdom worth £107 million in 1983; 47% up on four years earlier, with similar results evident in trade with other areas of the world. That brings even more merchant ships to the main Colombian ports of Barranquilla on the Caribbean and Buenaventura on the Pacific.

Buenaventura has had its bad reputation for some time although it is perhaps not fully justified today. The first recent report of an attack on an ocean-going merchantman was in July 1978 when the 12,147-ton *Banbury* was at anchor in the Roads waiting for a berth. As the master had previous experience of this port, he decided to mount a deck patrol. Nevertheless thieves got on board in the late evening and disappeared into no 1 hold. They were eventually spotted and chased off by the officers but managed to get away with ten cases of whisky and a photocopying machine. Five days later, after the ship had completed working cargo and was once again in the river waiting for the tide before sailing, an aggressive and well disciplined gang boarded at about 1930, armed with machetes and staves. They took one box of cargo from no 2 hold before being seen and then had a running battle with the majority of the ship's officers and crew in the course of which the master was injured by a knife wound in the stomach. The thieves made an orderly retreat with their loot and also with wrist-watches wrenched off the master and third officer.

There may have been many other similar incidents. However, the next recorded attack was made in December 1980 on the 16,199-ton cargo/container ship *Schwabenstein*, but no details are available. Three months later, the 14,620-ton *Mar Negro* was robbed on several occasions despite police being on board. Finally on leaving harbour they were boarded at 0215 in the buoyed channel by seven armed men in a fast launch who fired several shots to intimidate the crew. They then broke open a container full of hair-dryers and lowered 160 into their launch before leaving 20 minutes later. An attack took place on the 18,278-ton *Kubbar* at Buenaventura in December 1981, and another on the *Costa Andaluza* at nearby Cabo San Lorenzo in June 1982, but following these all has been quiet on Colombia's Pacific Coast, although no reason such as increased police activity has been found for this.

Further north, on the Caribbean coast is Barranquilla, a modern industrial city and Colombia's chief port. It is situated on the banks of the river Magdalena, ten miles from the sea and has a population of nearly 900,000. It has never been the site of any serious trouble apart from one reported attack on an ocean-going merchantman in June 1981. Other reports, both here and at the nearby port of Cartagena, have concerned small craft and are therefore covered in chapter 6.

Ecuador lies immediately to the south of Colombia on the Pacific coast and appears superficially to have the same factors of instability which could result in piracy in Colombia – military governments, tensions with her immediate neighbour (Peru), a poor but expanding economy with great inequalities between rich and poor and vast sparsely-inhabited areas of inaccessible forests. Surprisingly there is virtually no piracy. The American 14,515-ton general cargo vessel *Joseph Lykes* was boarded and robbed by pirates at Guayaquil in May 1982 but no other piracy reports of any nature have been received since.

From the absence of recent reports of attacks it can be assumed that both Ecuador and Colombia have overcome their one-time problem and ocean-going merchantmen are once again relatively safe. But until the reasons for this decline in attacks can be established, it is difficult to be certain that the peace will continue when the conditions of life so closely parallel those which give rise to piracy elsewhere.

Nevertheless it is entirely clear that, although ocean-going merchantmen may be safe, small craft and yachts certainly are not.

Brazil

Brazil provides an unexpected story. With 20 large ports, there seems no reason why Santos in the southern State of Sao Paulo should be the prime, if not the only, source of trouble for shipping. Together with Rio de Janeiro, it is one of the two leading ports and has a population of just over 400,000. It has expanded fast with development of Sao Paulo into the richest and most populous state in Brazil producing one-third of Brazil's coffee crop and two-thirds of its total manufactures. Four miles of docks can accommodate 50 ships at a time.

Santos is situated three miles up a narrow half-mile wide river amid broad sandy beaches which have also made it a popular tourist resort. Ship after ship has been attacked – the record is incomplete but it can be roughly estimated that there were at least 50 attacks between mid-1982 and the end of 1983. Since then attacks have continued, particularly against ships moored alongside as the police are believed to have the anchorage near the river mouth under firmer control than previously.

The first attack reported from Santos was on the 25,531-ton tanker *British Kennet* in June 1982. Whilst alongside Alemoa jetty, the master went into his cabin to find thieves and the whole room ransacked. He was immediately struck on the head, knocked down, and kicked in the ribs, then he was bound and a knife held to his face. He was dragged into the bedroom but remembers little else until the thieves left in a hurry and he was able to escape from his bonds. The alarm was raised by the chief officer who saw one thief carrying two suitcases past his cabin, but they threw their gear over the side into a rowing boat and disappeared. Though the ship's lifeboat was lowered to give chase, it did not catch them. The police were informed but no assistance materialised.

By the end of 1983, 32 cases of this nature had come to light in Santos but this appeared to be by no means the whole of the story. In September 1983 one local paper, *O Estado de Sao Paulo*, summarised 22 robberies which had taken place in the past eight months and stated that the International Shipping Federation had classified Santos as a dangerous port. In June 1983 the 38,711-ton bulk carrier *Benvorlich* was discharging cargo at a private terminal up a creek beyond the main port when she was boarded by robbers. Full details of the incident are given in chapter 7, but it is of interest that the master was informed later that there was then an average of one major shipboard robbery each night in Santos, though more usually in the main port or the waiting anchorage outside. He gave an interview for a television company who found shipboard robberies in Santos so frequent that they ran a special programme on the subject at peak viewing time each Saturday.

As elsewhere, the thieves are after cash and valuables and go direct to the master's cabin expecting to find the safe. Their methods are determined and ruthless but unsophisticated. In September 1983 the 77,961-ton bulk carrier *Angelic Protector* was berthed alongside discharging a cargo of potash. The chief officer heard noises from his cabin at about 2030 and went to investigate. Two men wearing nylon stocking masks over their faces put guns at his head and back, tied him up, and carried him into the master's cabin which had been ransacked. Other thieves were trying to open the safe with a hammer and iron lever and, when they did not succeed, they removed it bodily.

A year later, in September 1984, the master of another visiting vessel confirmed that several ships had been attacked in the roads, though not his own as he was invariably in ballast. Alongside the problem is greater as the robbers, in the absence of an alert deck watch and with the crew ashore, can creep aboard unnoticed. This master noted,

> There is no finesse. Robbers smash down doors and ports with jemmies and crowbars, demand the master open the safe and, if refused, belt him over the head with the bar! I know of one master who has died after such treatment.'

In the same month the Brazilian Naval Attaché in London said

> I would like to reassure you that the Brazilian authorities see these occurrences in the Port of Santos as acts of pure robbery, and I see no need whatsoever to explain their attitudes to you.

There is unfortunately no other evidence that this is the end of the story.

CENTRAL AMERICA

Apart from Mexico, Central America is in perpetual turmoil, many of its nations are plagued by war and experience constant intervention from America and Russia. Piracy as such does not, however, appear to exist though in such a politically volatile area the dangers of a peaceful merchant vessel getting mixed up in a war zone are obvious. Thus, in February 1983, two Nicaraguan fishing vessels operating in the Gulf of Fonseca on the Pacific coast of Honduras were attacked by El Salvadorean armed launches. A year later the *Ho Ming 7* was attacked by submersibles while loading sugar at Puerto Saudino in Nicaragua and in December 1983 the 9289-ton *Lionheart* was strafed by planes while 60 miles off Nicaragua.

An unusual case where the master showed quite exceptional initiative in saving his vessel occurred in January 1982 when the 9247-ton bulk carrier *Alta* was stopped off Puerto Cabezas on the eastern coast of Nicaragua, whilst making repairs to her engines. At about 1020 she saw a small motor boat approaching from a nearby cove with seven men aboard, four of whom were dressed in guerilla uniforms. She got underway as soon as she could and was moving by 1115, by which time the motor boat had closed to within 300 yards of the stern. The pirates started firing with small arms and this continued for half an hour, while the *Alta* tried to ram them. In doing this, the pirates were prevented from boarding astern because of the danger from *Alta*'s propeller and they finally departed at 1145, heading for another cargo ship anchored in the cove which they had probably taken over earlier. *Alta* subsequently discovered, amongst other damage, over 50 bullet holes and a number of broken window glasses.

Yet, provided ships avoid the known trouble spots of Central America and South America, there seems little for ocean-going merchantmen to fear throughout this area. Only Santos in Brazil remains the one area where robbery and violence predominate.

CHAPTER 6

Yachts And Small Craft

Yachts and small craft are easy targets for pirates. Yachtsmen in particular wander the far corners of the oceans alone, or anchor in quiet, secluded coves in apparently friendly neighbourhoods and in doing so make themselves vulnerable to attack by ordinary thieves or more determined pirates. They are particularly at risk in the vast waters of the Far East and the China Sea where, as described in chapter 4, some of the most callous pirates operate. Warnings have been given, too, of the dangers yachtsmen run off the Pacific coast of Colombia, despite the apparent fall in the number of attacks on ocean-going merchantmen. They are also at serious risk in the Caribbean, both in accidentally coming across drug smuggling rings which abound in this area and also cruising close to the shore in the apparent belief that this area is more peaceful than the developed European world. In brief, many yachtsmen lay themselves at risk through lack of thought and there is no central organisation to advise them of the dangers they may encounter. Because there are no comprehensive records of attacks it is extremely difficult to obtain an accurate picture of the situation. The incidents in the Log of Attacks have been gathered from many individuals and probably represent only a small part of the whole, but they are nevertheless sufficient to indicate quite clearly the extent and nature of the problem. Even within the more civilised waters of the United States, the US Coast Guard state 'Since mid-1973 hundreds of pleasure and fishing craft have disappeared in US coastal waters ...'

The Caribbean and Americas
The Caribbean, with its marvellous climate and many fascinating islands, is of particular appeal to yachtsmen who sail there in their thousands. It is a huge area, some 1500 miles from east to west, and 600 miles from north to south, bounded on the west by the Central American states of Mexico, Honduras, Nicaragua, Costa Rica, and Panama and, on the south, by Colombia and Venezuela. On the east, the West • Map p84–5 Indian islands of the Lesser Antilles lead up from Trinidad to the Virgin Islands and on to Puerto Rico, Haiti, the Dominican Republic, and Cuba and Jamaica, to complete the circle. The almost equally large Gulf of Mexico lies to the north through the Yucatan Channel while the Windward Passage between Cuba and Haiti gives access to the many islands of the Bahamas and to Florida. Thus small craft can pass with relative ease in short hops from the north coast of South America right up to Florida, relatively safe from detection and protected from the weather except in the hurricane season. The vast number of bays and coves provide great possibilities for secret activities and for eluding pursuit. These waters thus

appeal not only to holidaying yachtsmen, but also to drug smugglers who present one of the prime dangers in this area.

It is estimated that the drug trade into the United States of America is worth nearly $80 billion a year. Many of the drugs enter the US through Florida and the Gulf of Mexico. About 70% or more of the drugs exported are thought to originate from Colombia where cannabis and the coca tree grow naturally, and from where products can be brought north through the Pacific or the Caribbean. The drug trade has developed into an enormous business operating on an almost unprecedented scale.

However, it is not a business about which many facts are publicly available but one which has to be speculated on from the obvious end results and from the few cases which come to public light. In 1977 Captain Cope of the US Coast Guard studied drug smuggling at a time when there was a purported epidemic of yacht-jackings in US coastal waters. It is obvious that even he found it difficult to obtain hard facts on individual cases. However, his paper, 'Yachtjacking and the Coast Guard', concluded that half a dozen or so disappearances of yachts and small craft could be confirmed as hijackings and that these generally took place because the craft were suitable for drug trafficking.

The emergence of this type of drug trafficking was the result of an intensive law enforcement effort in the late 1960s and early 1970s which broke up the French–Corsican families who had previously been responsible for 70–90% of the heroin introduced into the United States. These organised rings were replaced by amateurs operating on both the east and west coasts in Central and South America. Initially they used aircraft and small fast boats to ferry the drugs but rising costs and dwindling supplies led to a decline in hard drug trafficking and a switch to the more easily obtainable marijuana, hashish, and cocaine. By mid-1972 large quantities were being transported and the amateurs began hijacking boats and thieving from one another.

In the early 1970s a pattern of losses of yachts and small craft began to evolve in the Lesser Antilles which run north from Trinidad to the Virgin Islands. Simultaneously, a significant amount of hard drugs began making their way from South America to the USA via the Lesser Antilles, Virgin Islands, and Puerto Rico. Later, as marijuana began to predominate, it was brought by sea through the Caribbean from Jamaica, Venezuela, and Colombia, and up the Pacific west coast of Central America. The smugglers needed craft capable of covering quite long distances without stopping to refuel and provision, and auxiliary powered sailing craft were one of their principal choices for hijacking. But the cargo-carrying limitations of these initiated a switch towards heavier displacement craft such as luxury yachts which not only were spacious, but were usually fitted with the latest in navigation equipment. Losses of this type of vessel therefore began to increase, particularly in the southern Caribbean.

In the Atlantic, the drug traffic route has generally been from the Caribbean coast of South America or Jamaica, through the Windward Passage east of Cuba into the Atlantic, and then via the Bahamas islands to the USA. This is the most direct course and navigation is considerably better than on the route to the Gulf of Mexico through the Yucatan Channel to the west of Cuba, where wind and current often combine to set on to the Cuban shore.

Much information on this subject has also been gathered from Tristan Jones, a yachtsman with vast sailing experience who lives aboard his trimaran *Outward Leg*, sails largely alone, and makes his living writing books. His experiences are numerous and have the ring of truth of one who has encountered circumstances face to face. He confirms that one principal source of drugs is still the Caribbean coast of Colombia, (as much as the Pacific coast), and from here drugs are smuggled to the Mexican Gulf coasts of the USA. Whole villages and families may depend entirely on the export of drugs for their livelihood. They ferry the goods out in small craft to larger 'mother ships' which steam away northward to feed, in turn, American small craft in the Gulf of Mexico or off the coasts of Texas and Louisiana. Hijacked yachts and small craft are often used as the 'mother ships', which explains why many boats have disappeared or been hijacked – the *Explorer II* seized off Colombia in 1981, the *Star III* attacked off Rio Hacha, Colombia in the same year, the *Saint Peter* seized at Barranquilla in 1981, and the *Susan Ann II* hijacked and taken to Cartagena in September 1981. A number of attacks continue to be on yachtsmen who have accidentally run into drug smuggling operations rather than on fishing craft and trawlers – in 1980 *Kalia III* was discovered in Norman Cay in the Bahamas with the owner dead in a dinghy riddled with bullet holes, the *Belle Esprit* was attacked by five speedboats off

Nassau in 1982, Pat and William Kemerara were murdered in the Exumas Islands when they stumbled across a drug transfer, the yacht *Snowbound* was attacked and shot up near Williams Island, a yacht was attacked 10 miles south of Santa Marte in Colombia and all on board were killed. It is clear that many such incidents occur at the beginning of the drug chain in Colombia or near its end towards the Bahamas. Nevertheless, the other West Indian islands and the Gulf of Mexico are not exempt from such dangers.

Thus those who approach the coast of Colombia should do so with considerable care. Where a whole village is involved in transporting drugs down to the coast for loading and obtains a large part of its livelihood from the drug trade, inhabitants hardly take kindly to strangers and any sign of possible interference. They may even capture a visiting yacht if it is long-legged enough and suitable for the drug trade. On the Pacific coast yachts may risk being stripped of everything of value and the crew being murdered if the vessel is not deliberately wrecked. The same risks apply to large areas of the Caribbean coast where the drug smugglers' main areas of activity are believed to be: the San Bernadino islands to the south-west of Cartagena, Barranquilla and the banks of the Magdalena river above the port, Tacanga about two miles north of Santa Marta, and Bahia Honda on the north-west coast of the Guajira peninsular. Tacanga is reputed to be the main exportation port for marijuana which is transported down the one road into the town in trailer-trucks whilst the beach is deserted of the usually ubiquitous customs officials, police and soldiers. It is loaded by the townspeople and children onto local craft shaped like dumb-barges and called 'bongos', and delivered to mother ships off shore.

The areas in the Bahamas which Tristan Jones believes are used for drug smuggling are: Norman Cay, Bimini, Gorda Key, Black Rock, Staniel Key, Derby Island, Georgetown, Hawk's Nest Creek, and certain parts of Andros Island. Despite the number of 'accidents' involving yachts which undoubtedly occur in this general area, there is no way of substantiating his statements.

However, not all the craft which have disappeared can be accounted for by attacks connected with the illicit drugs trade. Of the more than 600 fishing and pleasure craft which disappeared in US coastal waters between mid-1973 and mid-1977 it seems highly probable that only a few were hijacked and the disappearance of the remainder was due to some entirely different cause – most probably fraud or theft. The US Coast Guard are aware of only four confirmed hijackings since 1980, three occurring in the Gulf of Mexico and one in the Bahamas chain; three of these vessels were used for drug trafficking.

There are certain features which many of the small craft that are hijacked have in common. Generally they are well outfitted for a reasonably long voyage, are capable of carrying sizeable cargoes and are sometimes long-legged. There are often one or more hired crewmen on board with questionable identities; the owner may be known to be carrying a large sum of money, or valuables; and the boat may have left its port of departure without being observed and without reporting its intended movements. The US Coast Guard advise that yachts and small craft file a 'float plan' with someone they know and keep him advised of any significant change in the itinerary so that he can alert the coast guard if the craft does not arrive as expected. They also recommend that: ships travel in company with other vessels if possible; the background and identity of hired crew members should be checked carefully; yachts should clear with the local customs agent when outbound and give him a complete crew manifest and a list of all firearms and valuable property and portable equipment. If these precautions are taken the coast guard may have some hope of locating vessels in trouble. (See the appendix for details).

Small craft are attacked for countless other reasons and in many other areas – the Caribbean has no monopoly on violence. In the Caribbean there have been several cases, quite unrelated to the drug trade, of yachts being attacked whilst peacefully sheltering in coves and harbours. Horrifying though these attacks may be, they appear to be no more than the work of natives, possibly motivated by drink and drugs, who find an easy target which has moored without any of the precautions which it would be advised to take even in a European port. The yacht *Cheers* was attacked by an armed and naked Bequian in the Windward Islands in 1981; another was attacked at gunpoint in Castries harbour, St Lucia and a woman raped; and there have been other attacks of similar character. The attack on the yacht *Severance* in Antigua is described in more detail in chapter 7.

Other waters
Further afield yachtsmen could perhaps expect to be more

exposed to danger than when sailing in civilised popular holiday areas of the western world. It is abundantly clear that pirates in many places see yachts as easy prey and have little mercy. Peter Tangvald lost his wife in the Philippines in 1979 and the police then explained to him that it was normal pirate practice to kill all aboard and sink the yacht so as to leave no traces for the authorities. (See chapter 7 for more detail.)

Two years later the yacht *Edna Maree* was carrying fee-paying passengers off Pulo Lankani on the west coast of Malayia. Pirates swarmed on board from a Thai fishing boat. The Australian skipper, James Montgomery, threw the first into the water and pushed the second back into his boat. The third however stabbed him in the stomach and nearly cut off his right hand. Three pirates then raped one of the women passengers while the other woman escaped, together with her child, by hiding below decks.

• Map p82–3 The outcome can be very different if yachtsmen are armed and open fire in time. In 1979 the yacht *Kim* was in the Gulf of Thailand off Nakorn Si Thammarat. The police advised her that there were many pirates in the area whom they could not control so the yacht turned south for Songkhla. The owner was woken at about 0200 when a large grey boat came close alongside, shining two spotlights at the yacht. Two men armed with carbines stood on her upper deck ready to board and others stood by clearly prepared to support them. The yacht owner did not wait but opened fire with an AK47 automatic rifle, killed the two armed men, and sprayed the remainder with bullets. The attackers sheered off but the yacht rescued one wounded pirate from the sea who admitted that they were part of a protection racket of fishing boats in that area and run by a rich local landowner.

Another yacht was challenged that year in the same area at night. The two men on board switched on the spreader lights on the yard arm and allowed the light to reflect off their M16 rifle barrels while they sat on deck. They had no further trouble.

The lesson seems inescapable – that it is as well for small craft which are in the open oceans to arm themselves and to show their weapons long before any boat is allowed to come near them. Pirates are not merciful men, indeed if they were and their victims escaped, they would lay themselves wide open to subsequent prosecution by the police and could expect little mercy.

If yachtsmen wish to sail in these waters, then the risks must be recognised and steps taken to meet them. The evidence is very clear – the unarmed yacht is at serious risk wherever it sails, whether in the apparently civilised waters of the Caribbean or the more remote waters of the Far East. But there is no case on record of an armed yacht being overcome if it has displayed its armament in time.

CHAPTER 7

The Victims

The material in this chapter has been gathered from just a few victims' personal accounts of their experiences and illustrates the types of attack which have been, and still are occurring. Although there have been relatively few deaths or injuries, and no significant economic effects on the pattern of the world's merchant shipping, many have found the experience of being pirated very harrowing. The master of an ocean-going merchantman has every right to feel secure in his environment on board and can be rudely awakened when he discovers himself to be under attack, in familiar surroundings, and with no one aware of what is happening or of his need for help. The crew of a yacht can have their peace brutally interrupted by experiences which they will never forget. This chapter is an attempt to describe these events from the point of view of those who actually suffered. The accounts have been abridged and adapted a little but are, so far as possible, in the words of the victims.

OCEAN-GOING MERCHANTMEN
At sea

The 7621-ton Japanese tanker *Chie Maru* left Penang on 29 June 1983 after taking on palm oil. Two days later she was pirated in the Strait of Malacca. The following is a broad summary of a report by her master, Nagano Tomoaki, in the ship's log:

Thursday 30 June

When the ship left the west coast of Malaysia, the sea was very calm. Today at 2330 the master was attending to the ship's books, accounts, etc, and was due to go on the bridge before the ship entered the Phillip Channel. He lay down to get some rest. Two of the ship's mates came in so he chatted with them for a while. Then they went out and he asked them to

wake him up when they got nearer the position.
Friday 1 July

Whilst sleeping the master thought that he heard somebody opening the curtain on the door and he got up. The ship was then 13 nautical miles west of the Phillip Channel making nearly 13 knots in a moonlit flat calm sea, and the clock over his head showed that it was 0030. He wondered who had come in at such an odd time. As he drew the curtain, three men came in – one had a jack-knife and two had machetes. The man on the right lifted his machete, and the one on the left put his to the captain's throat, while the man with the jack-knife pushed it against the captain's stomach. Another man then came in and tried to tie up the captain's hands. The man on the right hand side used his machete to smash up the communication equipment.

The other machete-carrying pirate hit the captain in the left part of the back and the one carrying the dagger hit him on the head. He was tied up hands and feet. When the master asked 'Are you Indonesians?' they hit him, and when he asked 'Do you speak English?' they hit him again. He presumed this meant they didn't want him to speak out. And all the time the pirates spoke only with their hands and eyes.

Two coloured men watched the master while two others looked round his cabin. They snatched the master's watch and searched for a key with which to open some of the drawers and the safe but could not find it. They used hand signals to ask him if he had the key on him. The master replied 'No and I'm not going to tell you where it is.' He was hit with a machete.

The pirates tried the cabin key in the safe but it didn't fit so they hit the captain again, and then went on hitting him. Then they suddenly found the key behind his dictionary on the bookshelf – it will never be put behind the dictionary again!

They opened the drawers and found the master's wallet and some foreign currency, and also took an old watch. The safe had a combination lock which the captain changed periodically and supposed that the pirates would find it difficult to open – unfortunately however they managed it. As the pirates were about to leave, they pushed the master down again and covered him with a blanket but he managed to shake it off as they were leaving and he saw the third mate coming out of his cabin nearby. He shouted 'Danger! run for it!' and one pirate chased him [the third mate] briefly with his machete. Then the pirates disappeared into the crew's living quarters and were not seen again.

The master managed to release himself and went to the bridge where nothing was happening and no one had any idea of the struggle that had been going on down below.

These pirates had approached the ship on the blind side in a small fast boat and boarded aft by rope, and they left in the same way leaving the rope behind them. They were thought to be Indonesians aged between 25 and 30. All were barefoot and poorly dressed. Clearly they were highly nervous.

An attack in harbour

On 3 June 1983 the British *Benvorlich*, a 38,717-ton bulk carrier, was in Santos, Brazil, discharging bulk sulphur at a private quay away from the main port. Her master, Captain H H McIntosh was asleep in his cabin when he was woken at about 0200 by a crash as the door from the alleyway into the lobby of his quarters was broken open with a jemmy. As he switched on the bunk light he saw an evil-looking face above a revolver appearing round the doorway. Its owner indicated, finger to lips, that he was to keep quiet but Captain McIntosh, pretending not to understand, asked in a loud voice what they wanted while at the same time banging on his bulkhead to waken the radio officer next door – unfortunately a sound sleeper. The first intruder was joined by a second and they rapidly persuaded Captain McIntosh that silence was golden. Two more robbers also arrived and ransacked the day-room, indicated they wanted to know where the safe was and that they were after money. Captain McIntosh protested as loudly as he dared that he could not understand their demands, and had no money anyway. He was silenced by a blow with the revolver on the back of his head, dragged from his bunk into the day-room and spreadeagled on the deck. He was by now fully convinced that the jemmy would be used to 'persuade' him to show them where the safe was but at that point the robbers found it and so dragged the master back to his sleeping cabin and demanded the key. A knife prodding his back, and a cocked revolver at his temples were quite persuasive enough arguments.

The entertainments locker was also found and the thieves regaled themselves with rum and a fine malt whisky whilst they opened the safe. They found £2300 but ignored the medical drugs. They tied Captain McIntosh face down on his bunk, gagged him with his own necktie, and then left his cabin. He immediately tried to raise the alarm by banging with his heels on the bulkhead but they returned, threw him on the floor, hurled the whisky bottle at his head, and departed. Eventually the master succeeded in raising an alarm through the telephone but the thieves had escaped. The police seemed to treat this as a routine affair and a Lloyds surveyor, who had worked in the town for eight years, commented that Captain McIntosh was lucky to be alive as thieves usually did not hesitate to kill when they met with resistance. He still jumps at unusual noises.

YACHTS AND SMALL CRAFT

A Caribbean cruise

John and Susan Hutchinson went to the Caribbean in January 1984 looking forward to a splendid holiday to celebrate their silver wedding anniversary. Both were aged 47 - he was a British Airways Concorde pilot and she a State Registered Nurse and teacher until her marriage. They had chartered the yacht *Severance*, owned by Pat Tisdall who sailed her together with his girlfriend Sue Northcote. It sounded splendid and started just that way. After flying to Antigua, the Hutchinsons boarded the yacht and spent the first night quietly on board. The next day was enjoyably spent walking round English Harbour, Nelson's old base port.

The following day they moved out of English Harbour and pulled into Deep Bay in the afternoon, a local beauty spot and a perfect anchorage. Five other boats were there already. They had a drink and a barbecue in the stern before turning in early at about 9.30 pm. It was quiet and peaceful - just what they had hoped for.

Three hours later the cabin door broke open with a crash. A flashlight dazzled them and John Hutchinson found a shotgun in his face, and a knife at his throat. Two coloured men were in the cabin, clearly highly-charged by drink and drugs. 'Where's the cocaine? We want your drugs. Where are your guns?' started the older of the two. Meanwhile he took John's signet ring and Susan's watch to put in the pockets of his US Army battledress top. They tied up both John and Susan and then proceeded to tie Pat Tisdall to the mast on deck and Sue Northcote in the saloon. Shortly after they weighed anchor, started the engine and moved out to sea.

John and Susan remained tied up in the cabin and had time to think. Susan was sure that she was going to be raped; John was equally convinced. They thought about the motives of their attackers – were these men merely stealing the boat? Were they on a drugs run? Would they be dropped overboard? Together they decided that the best possible approach was to make it as easy for the two men as possible, not to resist and to be completely passive, and meanwhile to see where they could gain some advantage.

The engines stopped when they were about four miles out and the men came into the cabin. 'Hey, honky woman, have you ever had a black man?' Susan did not answer. John was cut free and pulled into the saloon where they tied him to the mast together with Sue, and then went back into the cabin.

Down below, the taller and older man used his long bladed knife to slash the nightdress off Susan and put her Harrods beach-bag over her head. When she pleaded and panicked at the thought of suffocating he took it partially off and then cut the bindings on her ankles.

Forty minutes later the second man came down and said 'Hey man, haven't you finished?' He put his gun down on the bunk and undressed. When it was all over they cut her free to let her go and wash. She picked up the sheet, wrapped it round her and went to the saloon.

The tall pirate, Jack, was being sick in the galley, full of drink and drugs. Susan, still well-controlled and looking for a possible advantage, put her arm comfortingly round him and sympathised. She persuaded him that Sue Northcote was a nurse and could look after him if she were released. Then she put on some clothes and all six sat in the cabin for the next three hours, with Pat Tisdall and John Hutchinson still tied up. But Susan had managed meanwhile to steal the bread-knife. It was a first step forward and little by little thereafter they improved their situation. John needed a drink so they eased the bonds tying his neck to the mast. Then he asked to go to the lavatory so they released him and fortunately forgot to tie him up when he returned. He lay face down on the bunk.

Dawn broke and Pat Tisdall was told to take the boat back to Deep Bay. The anchor was dropped at 6.45 am and the elder of the two raiders, now known to be called Cox, went ashore in the dinghy to get another man and said he would be back in a few hours with the guns and the drugs – clearly the yacht was to be used for a drugs run. Meanwhile Jack was left guarding the prisoners with a sawn-off shotgun.

This was clearly the only chance for the prisoners. John Hutchinson began to moan and writhe on his bunk. Susan insisted that it was a heart condition and Jack untied her so she could get the drugs from the medicine cabinet. While she gave them to John, she managed to pass him the concealed bread-knife. He faked another heart attack and Jack showed concern and bent over him. John burst off the bed with the knife and went for Jack who simply folded up. Susan ran for the radio and called 'Mayday Mayday!'

Then it all happened. A passing luxury yacht sent over an armed motor boat. Hundreds of Antiguans gathered on the beach while Susan came ashore to go to the hospital for examination. Statements were made to the police who took 2½ hours to arrive on the scene. Eventually Cox as well as Jack was arrested, though he is believed to have escaped later. The reports are that neither were locals but were visiting Jamaicans.

And the Hutchinsons? Never again will they believe that there is peace in the Caribbean on board a yacht. They too have learned the hard lesson of yachtsmen sailing in distant waters – that those who arm themselves are safe. Pat Tisdall had a rifle on board all the time – if only he had had it by him when it was needed.

A yachtsman's experiences

Peter Tangvald spent the typhoon season, in late 1978, holed up in the mangroves close to Cebu somewhere half-way in between Manila and Mindanao in the Philippines. He is one of those yachtsmen who perpetually cruise and love the sea. His yacht L'Artemis de Pytheas was an engineless 50-foot gaff schooner and his wife Lydia and 2¾-year-old son were with him.

In early February 1970 he sailed for Brunei and decided to cross the Sulu sea despite its evil reputation. It was the shortest and most peaceful route and promised a comfortable sail. But on the sixth day out they saw a small boat overtaking rapidly from astern. It was worrying and Lydia suggested taking out their single-barrelled shotgun and firing a warning shot but Peter thought it was too late already as the gun would have to be taken out from its storage place and loaded by which time the boat would be alongside. He hoped that the boat would turn out to be carrying fishermen, though if they were actually pirates, it would be best to allow them to take what they wanted and they didn't have many valuables anyway.

Unknown to him however, Lydia had taken out the gun and loaded it. As the boat drew alongside she fired a shot over their heads and warned them in English to sheer off. Almost immediately the pirates responded and shot her in the head; she fell overboard and the sea was stained with her blood.

A man came out of the pirate boat wheelhouse and levelled a gun at Peter Tangvald. Maybe because his young son Thomas was then clinging to his knee, maybe for some other reason, the pirate finally lowered his gun and sent two of his men on board. They took Tangvald's money and gun, and their boat speeded away and disappeared. Lydia was gone; even the large blood stained area where she had fallen into the sea had disappeared.

When Peter Tangvald eventually arrived in Brunei and the police carried out their investigation, they informed him that there were several hundred such attacks every year. He was lucky to be alive. His idea of non-resistance would have worked only with the less hardened pirates; more hardened ones would kill everybody on board and sink the boat to get rid of all traces of the attack. Nor would a mayday message have helped; the police simply did not have sufficient boats to be able to assist yachts in trouble on the high seas, though they might be able to help closer in to their bases.

Two years later he was attacked again, this time by three men who boarded his yacht at anchor in Gabes, Tunisia. On that occasion, although badly beaten up, fortunately no-one was killed, but there were some nasty moments. The pirates were caught later.

He tells also the story of his friend Jean-Charles who was anchored south of Borneo in 1978 when he was woken by a man sitting on his chest holding a long knife across his throat. Two other men emptied the boat completely while he lay there – the clothes, the sails, the engine unbolted from its bearers. But they left him alive and he too was lucky.

He also recalls George whose boat was boarded by two intruders one night whilst at anchor off the west coast of Africa. One tripped and woke him up. George shot both dead with the revolver he kept under his pillow and, fearing that the local police might react against him when they heard, set sail and dumped the bodies in deep water in the Atlantic. François, an ex-French legionnaire, ignored the ban on arms imposed by eastern countries and even carried hand grenades. Once he threw one of these clear across the deck of a boat which was coming alongside to board – they lost no time in sheering off.

The need to be alert

In 1980 Michael Burdick and two others chartered a Peterson 44, the *Grand Cru*, to cruise the Caribbean. They thought they would be prepared for anything and their initial outfitting included an 8mm high-powered hunting rifle and a .32 automatic pistol, though only Michael Burdick himself had previous experience with firearms. Piracy was routine cocktail party conversation but they thought themselves well prepared.

One Saturday afternoon on their initial shakedown cruise they had left Holmes Cay in the Bahamas and were *en route* for Chub Cay, a small collection of sparsely populated islands. They were running with the wind and goosewinging; the islands were encompassed by a shimmering blue horizon. A solitary fishing smack, with its white hull resting listlessly on the water added to the perfection, and the warmth of the sun and the excitement of a year cruising the Caribbean created an unsurpassably exhilarating atmosphere.

Apparently out of nowhere, four Bahamians approached in a 16-foot skiff and offered to help sail the boat. Michael Burdick quickly declined, the skiff left quietly and no-one thought further about the incident. Twenty minutes later however, four men dressed in dark blue jump-suits approached in a skiff. They came to within fifteen yards off the port side, and claimed, in authoritative voices, with a heavy island accent, to be police. They stated that the *Grand Cru* had been under surveillance for several hours, that her low waterline was indicative of drugs on board, and they wished to search the boat. Several men began talking at once shouting 'Stop the boat, turn off the diesel, stop the boat! Where is everyone? Get everyone on deck!'

In the first moments of confusion, everyone tried to give polite answers. One crew member in the after cabin had his pistol in hand but hesitated at what to do. The skipper asked to see the Bahamians' official identification but they angrily retorted 'We don't need no papers, we're police.' Meanwhile the skiff moved in closer and automatic rifles were aimed at Burdick and his crew. Three men came on board with guns in hand while the fourth remained at the helm of the skiff. They ordered the sails to be lowered.

The leader continued barking questions 'Where are the drugs? Where is the coke? Where are your guns?' Progressively they seemed to accept the explanation that there were no drugs and contented themselves with stealing the guns and all available cash, only firing at the skipper, and narrowly missing, when he moved too fast and unexpectedly for them. They left without firing another shot and repeatedly threatened 'Don't go to Nassau or we'll kill you in the street with your own guns'.

This cost the *Grand Cru's* crew $300 and their guns but many would say how lucky they were not to suffer anything worse. In retrospect, had they shown their guns in advance, the Bahamians would not have come alongside. It was only their slow reactions and comparative inexperience with firearms that allowed the raiders to succeed with the attack.

CHAPTER 8

Maritime Terrorism

On 21 February 1982 the 1843-ton coaster *Saint Bedan* entered Lough Foyle on her way to Londonderry some 20 miles further up. Lough Foyle lies between Northern Ireland and Eire and, as is normal practice, merchant ships have to carry a pilot when close inshore. They embark from the pilot station which is at Moville near the entrance to the Lough in Eire.

On this occasion, as was usual, the pilot cutter came out • Map p88–9 from Moville and one man came on board the coaster. Nothing appeared untoward – everything seemed quite normal. But as the 'pilot' reached the bridge, he produced a pistol and held up the master, Captain Roderick Black. Six more men, all hooded and masked, swarmed on board armed with sub-machine guns and pistols, and rounded up the crew.

The master was forced to anchor about one mile off the Eire coast and the crew were ordered to take to the life rafts. Some of the raiders disappeared into the engine room with five bags of explosives. A few minutes later they left the vessel and arrived at Moville pier just as the shore staff, who had been gagged and bound, had managed to release themselves and were about to raise the alarm. At that moment the charges exploded and *Saint Bedan* disappeared in 40 feet of water. The raiders too were never seen again.

That was the second such novel terrorist attack in Northern Ireland. Just over one year earlier the 1393-ton coaster *Nellie M* had been sunk in a similar manner in Lough Foyle when an Irish Republican Army (IRA) gang of 12 held up the Moville pilot station. While five of the gang remained in command of the pier, the remaining seven forced the pilot to take them out to the ship and they went on board. The crew was set adrift in a dinghy and *Nellie M* too was blown up and sank.

Such terrorist attacks are clearly not the sole prerogative of Northern Ireland. The Polisario guerillas operate from Algeria and lay claim to the Western Sahara which was taken over by Morocco in 1976. Morocco now operates a line of defence against these guerillas across the northern half of the Western Sahara through Laayoune, Bu Craa, and Smara. The guerillas hold most of the desert to the south of this and have renamed this area the Democratic Saharan Arab Republic. Meanwhile Moroccan, Spanish and Portuguese trawlers fish off the Western Sahara shores where the waters are rich in sardines. It is not surprising that they should be targets for the Polisario guerillas; nine attacks were reported between 1980 and 1983 (see the Log of Attacks). A further two attacks were made on Cuban supply vessels near Villa Cisneros in 1980 by unidentified war planes – possibly an attempt by the Moroccan government to interrupt supplies to the guerillas.

There have been eleven attacks recorded in the Lebanon – an obvious offshoot of the state of perpetual war in that country. In Spain, Basque guerillas have claimed responsibility for several attacks of a relatively sophisticated nature, on two occasions using magnetic mines and on another exploding a device on board a Spanish destroyer. Guerillas, including the Moro National Liberation Front and the Communist New People's Army, have attacked small ships in the Philippines area. Other attacks have taken place along Nicaragua's Pacific and Caribbean coasts, as discussed in chapter 5. In addition to all these incidents there have been many air launched missile attacks on merchant ships proceeding along the Arabian Gulf, mines laid in the Red Sea, and attacks on yachts entering Eritrean waters.

However, this book is intended as a commentary on piracy rather than terrorism and it is not appropriate to attempt any detailed discussion of these attacks. Indeed, any analysis would no doubt show nothing other than a predictable trend – that the targets are generally chosen on purely political grounds, with as much importance attached to a ship's nationality as to its value or any other factor. The danger of terrorist attack occurrence can be assessed with comparative ease by anyone who makes even a superficial study of the world's political trouble spots. There is no advice to offer to the ship owner other than to keep away.

CHAPTER 9

The Law and Action By World Authorities

Law develops in the light of past history and subsequent interpretations of judges which establish precedent. Circumstances may change, but the law never looks forward, only back, and it may take many years to change. It by no means follows therefore that today's law meets today's circumstances; in most cases it does not. Nor is there any international law to which all nations subscribe formally other than by custom. Most countries have their own national laws and many their individual interpretations of international law. It is therefore very difficult to be precise on exactly where the law on piracy stands. Moreover law needs to be backed up by force if it is to be effective, but there is no single authority, nation, or consortium of nations, which is responsible for discipline on the high seas.

The concept of piracy as an international crime is an ancient one. As long ago as 1668 Sir Leoline Jenkins declared that 'All pirates and sea rovers are outlawed ... by the law of all nations. That is, out of the protection of Princes and of laws whatsoever.' For centuries, the pirate has been regarded a common enemy. Precise legal definitions of piracy today are enshrined in the Geneva Convention on the High Seas of 1958 which declared it to be:

Any illegal acts of violence, detention, or any act of depredation committed for private ends by the crew or passengers of a private ship or a private aircraft, and directed: (a) On the high seas against another ship or aircraft, or against persons or property on board such ship or aircraft; (b) Against a ship, aircraft, persons or property in a place outside the jurisdiction of any state.

One essential feature of this definition is that piracy is something committed for 'private ends'. Terrorism in support of political objectives is not therefore piracy; nor can piracy be committed by a warship or a government ship or aircraft even if the act is unauthorised. The Draft Convention prepared by the Third United Nations Conference on the Law of the Sea in 1982 (UNCLOS 1982) also states, in Article 101 that

... on the high seas or in any other place outside the jurisdiction of any State, every State may seize a pirate ship or aircraft, or a ship taken by piracy and under the control of pirates, and arrest the persons and seize the property on board. The courts of the State which carried out the seizure may decide upon the penalties to be imposed ...

The punishment of pirates is therefore left to the discretion of individual states; any nation may arrest a pirate and try him according to its own laws.

Though at first glance this may appear straightforward, the situation rapidly becomes more complex once one examines the precise interpretation of what appear to be simple words. What, first of all, are the 'high seas'? The interpretation may vary from nation to nation.

So far as the United Kingdom is concerned, precedent was created when a collision occurred in the Straits of Dover in 1876 less than two miles off the coast, causing fatal casualties. The master of one of the ships, a German citizen, was charged in the British courts with manslaughter. The decision was then that the sovereignty of the Queen stops at the low water mark and this concept was subsequently enshrined in the Territorial Waters Jurisdiction Act of 1878. In British law therefore, all waters outside the low water mark are 'high seas'. Internationally, this concept was reiterated in the United Nations Convention on the Law of the Sea 1958, Article 1. The simple and currently correct definition is contained in *Archbold's Criminal Pleading, Evidence and Practice in Criminal Cases,* (published by Sweet and Maxwell, 41st edition, 1982). In the case of *R v Liverpool Justices ex P Molyneux (1972)* it was held that 'high seas' has the same meaning as when used with reference to Admiralty jurisdiction, ie 'all oceans, seas, bays, channels, rivers, creeks and waters below low water mark and where great ships go, except such parts of oceans, etc, as lie within the body of a country.'

Unfortunately, however, UNCLOS 1982 effectively excluded Exclusive Economic Zones from the definition of high seas and these, in many cases, reach out to 200 miles from shore. The United Kingdom has not yet ratified that Convention; nor are insurance companies anxious to forecast the effect of such a ratification on policies. Since then however Mr Justice Staughton stated in June 1982, in the case of the *Andreas Lemos*, that he saw no reason to limit piracy only to acts outside territorial waters, which implies the complete reverse of the UNCLOS view, at least so far as British law is concerned. The precise definition of high seas and piracy therefore appears vague and undecided but according to the judgement above, nations would seem to have at least some right to intervene in other nations' territorial waters if there is a piratical act there.

It has nevertheless been accepted so far, that each nation is responsible for control of its own waters. Singaporean patrols do not penetrate Indonesian waters; no foreign warship has come to the aid of the many ships pirated in Nigerian waters. But legally it seems acceptable to go to the aid of a ship which has been attacked by anyone for 'private ends' and which is anywhere below the low water mark (where by definition all ocean-going ships must be). This may well become necessary since the waters where piracy is occurring are the very same waters where the indigenous defence forces and navies tend to be small or non-existent.

World Authorities

Since the dissolution of Pax Britannica and the decline of the British and other European empires, no single world authority has emerged which has both the power and the will to control piracy. In my extensive research I have not even come across any authority which has a full list of attacks on merchant shipping in recent years. Attitudes appear to be hardening and pressures could be brought to bear, with constructive results. It was thus external pressures on the Nigerian government which first led to their setting up patrols against piracy and similar pressures led to the institution of the Thai anti-piracy programme, limited though it may be.

However, today's maritime organisations are essentially

advisory rather than disciplinary. Most trading nations have one or more national organisations who concern themselves with shipping and its problems, though again only in an advisory capacity; their role is to represent the unified views of shipowners. In the United Kingdom one such body is the General Council of British Shipping (GCBS), another is the Working Group on Armed Robberies from Merchant Ships (originally the West African Monitoring Group), comprising representatives from government, shipowners and unions; in Germany, Der Bundesminster Für Verkehr; in Norway the Maritime Directorate; in the United States of America, the Bureau of Shipping; in France the Comité Central des Armateurs de France – there are also many other similar bodies. Each of these organisations can make representations to its own government and also to the International Maritime Organisation (IMO) which has headquarters in London.

The IMO first became effective in March 1958 with an initial membership of 21 countries, which has since expanded to 127. It is a specialised agency of the United Nations Organisation, and deals exclusively with all matters related to the safety of international shipping, the promotion of high maritime standards and efficiency in navigation, and with the prevention and control of pollution of the marine environment by ships. It is highly unlikely that anyone envisaged piracy as a major problem when it was first formed but it has nevertheless gradually widened its scope to cover the whole field of piracy and fraud in the maritime environment. Even today it has no formal powers of enforcement but its function is becoming more important and its influence increasing. Nevertheless, it remains no more than an advisory body and ultimately action is the responsibility of the governments concerned.

In 1983 the General Assembly of IMO adopted a series of resolutions encouraging member governments to take steps to suppress piracy, to report any measures taken, and also to report on any incidents involving their ships. This was as a result of gradually increasing concern amongst shipowners who saw the problem of piracy mounting world wide, particularly in West Africa and around Singapore. This appears to be the first move made by any international body towards even the first essential step of compiling a central register of attacks; important since little is likely to happen to counter piracy until there are some fairly comprehensive statistics available which prove that piracy is a *real* problem and not just some master's nightmare. Work has begun on creating this and in July 1984 the International Maritime Bureau had the information to be able to report to the IMO that piracy was decreasing but that there was some concern about the situation in South America. Unfortunately, the records obtained to date are far from complete and the number of attacks last reported to the IMO in July 1984 were substantially fewer than those listed even in this book. However, the central register is a beginning and should grow and it has enabled the IMO to publish recommended steps to be taken to deter pirates. The International Shipping Federation (ISF) has also issued a list of preventive measures known to be adopted by some shipowners in countering attacks. So too have the Baltic and International Maritime Conference (BIMCO), the government of the Federal German Republic, and the Swedish Shipowners' Association. (These are commented on in chapter 10).

Day-to-day research on piracy is largely conducted by the International Maritime Bureau. This, again, is an advisory rather than an executive body, sponsored by the International Chamber of Commerce (ICC) who work very closely with the IMO. They are based in the outskirts of London and are charged with the investigation of maritime fraud and piracy. They keep track of all reported incidents and have produced two reports on the situation analysing the causes and the trends, giving statistics, and offering advice to shipowners as well as advice on marine policing.

The United Nations Conference on Trade and Development (UNCTAD) have also concerned themselves with the problem, notably in their inter-governmental meeting at Geneva in February 1984 when they studied means of combating fraud and piracy. Their examinations were largely concerned however, with the application of existing and future international law, rather than with more immediate practical steps.

Outside of these types of organisation there are several organisations which concern themselves more specifically with the humanitarian aspects of the problem, and their principal concern is refugees. One such body is the International Committee of the Red Cross. They have no more legal right than any other committee to transgress against the laws of a state or to interfere in its internal affairs in order to pursue their aims. But they nevertheless manage to work in the close interests of refugees, particularly in the Gulf of Siam. In the same field there is the United Nations High Commission for Refugees (UNHCR) based in Geneva which is the principal organisation concerned with events in the Gulf of Thailand and other refugee problems around the world. Faced with the appalling statistics for attacks in the Gulf of Thailand, they appointed a team of three experts in 1983 to examine the problem in general and make recommendations. These are now being pursued in collaboration with countries in the region. One of the most important concerned the setting up of a regional centre to co-ordinate information concerning pirates and their activities. The centre will be of enormous value, and illustrates one of the unfortunate facets of the whole subject of piracy already mentioned – that no individual or agency has enough information to accurately assess the scale of the problem.

The Log of Attacks lists a great many incidents and possibly forms the most exhaustive list in existence. But it is also quite likely that it represents at the most no more than half of the actual number of attacks. Many incidents are not reported, partly due to lack of communication, and partly due to reluctance on the part of some shipowners to report them in order to avoid bad publicity, increased insurance premiums, trouble with unions, or offending the authorities in whose waters the incident occurred and to where the company wishes to continue sending ships. Add to this the lack of accurate statistics, the lack of co-ordinated international policy for practical policing or protection, and a natural unwillingness to interfere with ships of other flags, and it becomes obvious that the pirate has less to fear than should be the case.

So there is a vast gap between the international committees who consider the problem, and the practicalities of the situation faced by the seaman who is under attack, whether he be the master of an ocean-going merchantman, or skipper of a private yacht. No one organisation has power in this area although many have advisory capabilities and can bring considerable pressure to bear. Ultimately the only significant authority rests with each nation which has direct responsibility for its own territorial waters. Pressure can be put on governments by these international organisations, though it is more likely to be the prospect of financial losses which result in action. If insurance rates rise, this will mean increased cost to merchant shipping; if ships refuse to berth because of the danger, then this will be financially detrimental to the nation concerned. Short of another Pax Britannica, nothing else seems likely to cure today's situation. Yet it is ironic that a handful of largely uneducated poor young men can hold the world's shipping to ransom in such fashion.

CHAPTER 10

Precautions for Ship and Yacht Masters

There are several steps to consider in organising a ship's defences against piracy, quite apart from those which should be taken by national authorities on shore. All of these are obvious and relatively simple but deserve deep thought and a logical approach to make them successful. It is not, however, possible to do more than indicate the general lines which precautions should take, since they will vary from ship to ship and from area to area depending on the level of the potential threat. Each individual needs therefore to think out a strategy applicable to his particular circumstances. The most difficult task is assessing the level of threat to be expected since there can be no guarantee that piracy will remain at today's low level but could well escalate rapidly. Better defences may well become necessary almost overnight.

OCEAN-GOING MERCHANTMEN

The International Maritime Bureau have published details of the precautions recommended by the Baltic and International Maritime Conference and the International Shipping Federation and these are listed in the appendix. They consist largely of those steps which can be taken with relative ease without additional equipment. Various commercial private security firms offer programmes for shipowners desiring an improved level of defence. These start with training of a ship's crew in defence and progress to the application of special additional equipment. The objectives of a typical programme are listed in the appendix.

The principle steps which should be taken fall into the following categories:

- Avoidance of attack.
- Obtaining adequate warning of attack.
- Measures to prevent boarding.
- Minimising losses after being boarded.

Avoidance of attack

It is obvious that the best way of avoiding attack is to keep clear of those areas where it seems most likely to occur. One or two ships do precisely that and trade with Nigeria did suffer slightly during the worst periods of piracy in her waters. But it is not a realistic solution since shipping companies have to follow trade if they are to remain in business and, since piracy follows trade, the two most inevitably meet.

Virtually all attacks have taken place in the dark with the exception of one or two flagrantly open attacks in West African waters. Ships are therefore advised to keep clear of known pirate areas by night. The passage of the Malacca Strait, particularly south of Singapore, should be made by day. In West Africa it is sensible to proceed to sea at night, standing as far off as possible while still remaining in VHF radio contact with the shore. It is more difficult to put to sea again once berthed alongside than when waiting in the roads, though alongside at least, (despite the current experience of Santos), one is nominally under the eye of the shore authorities and there are opportunities to hire guards.

But the steps which some masters have taken of moving 15 miles or so off the West African coast and steaming overnight without lights could possibly lead to worse disaster. There is obviously a sensible position to be taken between avoiding danger and risking yet worse loss.

One other means of avoiding attack is worthy of mention: the hiring of shore-based security guards. The employment of groups such as the 'bow and arrow' men of Nigeria have a marked deterrent effect even if their arrows have never yet found a target. If they are a part of the same protection racket as a group of pirates, the fact that they have been hired will at least have bought that particular pirate gang off and the ship will remain protected against rival gangs.

Obtaining adequate warning of attack

Radar is of some help but tends to be swamped by a mass of

small echoes in the crowded waters where piracy usually occurs. At sea, radar targets are often obscured in the vital stern sector where pirate craft normally approach. There is little substitute for an alert lookout who can be aided by good lighting by, for example, keeping the cargo working lights on overnight. A searchlight or an Aldis lamp is useful for illuminating suspicious movements. The deck watch has to be strengthened as much as possible – it is extraordinary in the records in this book on how many occasions ships have been surprised by attack even when they had what they believed to be an adequate deck watch. That watch then has to have some means of raising the alarm, whether it be by the ship's whistle or by walkie-talkie. The ship's whistle is usually the most readily accessible means of doing this. Ideally too it should be possible to check that the watch is still active lest they have been surprised and intruders are already on board.

Measures to prevent boarding

The most obvious steps are to seal the hawsepipes with fitted plates and to give the watch on deck knives with which to cut the grapnel lines thrown up by intruders. Pirates have generally climbed on board ships berthed alongside by such means rather than, for example, trying to rush the gangway – a method which perhaps seems to be a little too blatant, even in areas where there is no opposition from the shore authorities. Some simple weapons have also been found to be most effective, particularly the use of ships' signal cartridges and Very light pistols. Empty beer bottles filled with sand which can be stacked on deck ready to hurl at intruders are also extremely effective. Perhaps less practical is the use of hoses since many intruders would regard the thought of a shower in the tropics with pleasure, but they can be effective if the force of the water is sufficient to knock an attacker off a shaky hold on the ship's side or on a grapnel and line. However, the delay involved in starting up a ship's fire pumps is quite unacceptable and they would need to be kept running continuously to be of any real use.

Yet despite taking these precautions many have been surprised at the extreme agility of young barefoot pirates. One commercial company offers detachable barbed wire which can be installed round the gunwale, or just over the poop area when on passage and likely to be attacked from aft. It is a simple yet clearly effective defence.

Minimising losses after boarding

The watch must alert the crew to the fact that the ship has been boarded. Provided the crew retreats into the accommodation areas, bridge structure and engine room through specifically designated entrances they have a chance of remaining unharmed while the pirates raid the cargo. All but these designated entrances should be securely closed during a ship's time in port and in dangerous waters in order to minimise the chances of one being carelessly left open. At sea, in areas where piracy is likely, it is highly advisable that the bridge team lock themselves in so that safe navigation is possible even when the ship is under attack. It is however remarkable how many attacks at sea have taken the crew by total surprise and in how many cases the master was either in, or just near his cabin and the bridge quite unsecured.

There are a great number of other steps which can be taken to make the pirates' task more difficult. Storeroom doors can be tack-welded shut with short lengths of piping; cheap padlocks can be replaced by others which are less susceptible to bolt cutters; hatches must be closed; at night, accommodation entrances must either be guarded or secured as much as possible so that pirates cannot gain easy access.

Commercial solutions

These measures discussed above are simple solutions and their implementation would probably considerably reduce the incidence of successful pirate raids. However, commercial firms offer more sophisticated and highly effective defences such as trip wires on deck which set off stun packages, and portable barbed wire defences. The essence of prevention is to make the pirates' task as difficult as possible yet a majority of shipowners still rely on such simple approaches as locking money and drugs in a safe which is always in the master's cabin, not bolted down, and with the keys easy to discover. However, when deciding what steps to take it is worth noting that today's pirates are, for the most part, relatively simple men and can be easily discouraged. But they learn quickly and tomorrow's pirates could be very different.

Firearms

The use of firearms in merchant ships is a very questionable principle. So far as British merchant ships are concerned, their carriage is governed by the Explosives Act of 1897 and the

Firearms Act of 1968 which state very broadly that firearms carried as 'ship's equipment' may be retained on board in the care of the master but that all others are subject to the usual statutory regulations. The most common advice however is not to carry firearms because the dangers which may arise from their possible misuse are at least as great as the advantages which they might bring. Firearms are tricky things; they need to be used by trained men and in the wrong hands can create more trouble than they solve – friends may be shot rather than pirates. And in the last resort if a pirate is shot, will it be seen as an act of self-defence, or murder or manslaughter in the eyes of the law of that particular country? Better, many think, to avoid their use altogether.

YACHTS AND SMALL CRAFT

Yachts and small craft are infinitely more vulnerable than ocean-going merchantmen. Some advice from the US Coast Guard, in whose area hundreds of pleasure craft have disappeared, is contained in the appendix, but apart from this no central organisation exists to advise owners in the same way as with merchant shipping. The steps which yachts and small craft need to take can however be analysed in similar categories, though arriving at different conclusions because of their much smaller size.

Avoidance of attack

It is far more important for yachtsmen completely to avoid attack than it is for larger merchantmen who are more able to mount adequate deck watches and obtain warning of what is coming.

The avoidance of attack must be a major part of a yacht's defences if only because it is so small and unprotected. Nor is there usually anyone to whom a yachtsman can turn to in trouble, unless he happens to be lucky enough to be near a police boat or a helpful warship. Even if he sends a radio message, help will usually still be out of sight by the time the pirates have finished their work and left. In many areas there is no help to be sent since the shore authorities may have insufficient craft or even none at all.

It is obvious that to avoid attack yachtsmen must keep clear of areas in which pirates are known to operate. The ocean areas where yachtsmen are particularly at risk are the Far East, particularly in the Gulf of Siam, the Sulu and Celebes

Seas, and at the two ends of the drug smuggling chain as it passes through the Caribbean, as well as off the Pacific coast of Colombia. But there is an important second requirement: not to lay oneself open to attack even in the most apparently peaceful spot. To secure to the shore in a deserted and peaceful cove with palm trees waving and a silver moon is an idyllic dream too easily shattered. It is extremely foolish yet hundreds of yachtsmen do it every day.

Obtaining adequate warning of attack

By day it is possible to obtain good warning of the approach of pirates merely by keeping a good look out, but at night the problem is an entirely different matter. Constant watch on radar is a partial solution. It is possible to buy intruder alarms which will either sense persons on deck or small craft coming in close, but they are likely to be a severe drain on a yacht's relatively small battery power. There is no adequate solution by night other than to rig trip wires on deck or resort to the older fashioned method of scattering tin tacks to deter barefoot intruders. The crew will then normally be below, particularly when in harbour, and any noise on deck will alert them quickly. Certainly a few seconds warning before the crash as the door is kicked in could be vital.

Measures to prevent boarding

If pirates can be seen in time, then it is fundamental that they should know how they will be received. Peter Tangvald, who so tragically lost his young wife, has clearly thought deeply about this. He believes that a yacht should have a high-powered rifle which could be used to fire a warning shot at an approaching boat while it is still at a distance, is not finally committed to an attack, and has time to sheer off. To that one could add, as I am sure Michael Burdick would after being surprised in the *Grand Cru*, that it is essential to be determined, to act quickly, and to show no sign of indecision. There are many cases in this book, and probably many others which have been unreported, which show that the yachtsman who shows he is armed at an early stage succeeds in defending himself; the others do not. Tristan Jones, as mentioned below, argues that firearms are unnecessary and he prefers to have a cross-bow on board. Others prefer the more radical solution of automatic rifles as on the yacht *Kim* in the Gulf of Siam but this choice is perhaps a little excessive for the majority.

Defences against attack and firearms

Unlike merchant ships with high freeboards there is no possibility of delaying the boarding of pirates who have come close to a small craft. Normally they will outnumber a defending yacht's crew. Should one accept their boarding quietly and passively and hope to stay alive even if they do strip the yacht bare, or hope to be able to turn the tables and gain advantage as John and Sue Hutchinson did when they were attacked in the yacht *Severance*? Or is the only answer to risk everything and fight?

There are many arguments and counter-arguments. Some believe firmly that any sign of resistance merely encourages pirates to show greater cruelty; others that to reply in kind is the only possible solution. The answer was perhaps indicated when Peter Tangvald spoke with the police in Sabah who told him quite clearly that a vast majority of pirates would insist on destroying every trace of their victim thus eliminating evidence that might lead to their capture. Without question many of the attacks on yachts have been extremely violent – James Montgomery had his hand nearly hacked off, yachts have fallen foul of the Caribbean drug smuggling rings, attempted attacks have been made on yachts in the Gulf of Siam, and so on. Fighting back would seem to be the only answer and if one is to fight, then one must prepare for it properly.

In deciding how to fight it is essential to remember that pirates usually attack without warning, either by night when a small yacht is unlikely to have a deck watch, or in stealth by day. A yacht's crew must therefore be prepared to act extremely quickly and, in addition to a long-range defence weapon to warn pirates off they need rapid reaction short-range weapons for fighting at close quarters. George (who was mentioned in chapter 6) kept a revolver under his pillow with which he was able to kill two intruders when one tripped and woke him at night. Another solution is to keep a small knife handy to pick up naturally as one goes down the companion way and to keep mini-flares down below which can be lethal at short range. Rifles are not practical because of the difficulty of handling such weapons rapidly in a small confined space.

There are therefore sound grounds for believing that yachtsmen need both a long-range defence weapon to warn pirates off and a good rapid re-action short-range system. Such weapons do not necessarily have to be firearms, though many yachtsmen carry them. However, the use of firearms in small craft is arguably more acceptable than in large ocean-going merchantmen, not only because they are more at risk and easier for pirates to overwhelm if they are not properly armed, but also because it is more viable to train adequately a small crew in the use of firearms. However, the veteran Tristan Jones who sails a 36-foot trimaran *Outward Leg* is dead-set against the carriage of firearms. They bring difficulties with customs officials and it is even possible that their discovery, if they are not declared, could lead to imprisonment and confiscation of the boat. There are other dangers too. Even if the yacht's crew are fully trained, firearms can be used too easily against the wrong people. Not every boat which approaches is a pirate craft; the first which approached Michael Burdick after his attack gave every sign of being another pirate boat but turned out to be a fisherman who wanted some propellor grease.

Tristan Jones' prime solution for long-range defence is the cross-bow rather than the gun. Cross-bows can be lethal and are not subject to customs restrictions. In England the smallest target cross-bow, accurate to some 15 metres range, costs less than £20 and fires a steel-tipped plastic bolt which is quite sufficient to do severe damage to a man. No licence is required to buy one. Larger cross-bows have a much greater range and effect. And if visiting foreign parts where there are some suspicions about the natives, it does no harm to be seen practising on the beach, so that every one is aware of what they might meet with if they came on board unexpectedly.

For the shorter-range weapon, despite his disapproval of firearms, he has a number of very effective alternatives all of which are designed to overcome potential difficulties with the customs. One is a metal sleeve which fits into the barrel of a flare gun to enable it to fire standard .35 ammunition. Although this is an effective firearm, it is extremely unlikely that it could be discovered by any normal customs inspection provided it had been dismantled on entering harbour. Another is a portable flame thrower which weighs no more than 40 pounds and yet has an effective range of up to 40 yards. Molotov cocktails are made up easily from glass bottles and gasoline with a rag in the bottle mouth and can be hurled a considerable distance. And finally, if one is boarded, it is useful to have a bottle of drugged or poisoned whisky handy so that the invaders can be invited for a drink!

Each yachtsman has his personal view on the subject though certainly many yachtsmen feel the need to be armed for adequate security.

CHAPTER 11

Where Next and Why?

Pirates today have little in common with those of the old days. There is still of course the eternal theme of money, but the mythical romance we attach to these characters bears little relevance to contemporary piracy. Modern pirates vary in type from the callous men who prey on the Vietnamese boat refugees; to the hardened criminals who engage in drug smuggling from South America to the United States or those who are merely young, ignorant, and poor and seek relatively quick and easy gain at the expense of the wealth of the developed world's merchant shipping.

The incidence of all these types of piracy has implications for the more developed world. Although developed nations have the power to deal with threats to law and order on their home ground (for instance with drug smugglers), it is an entirely different story when they are faced with piracy overseas beyond their spheres of control.

Fifty years ago the world was largely dominated by European empires, with Britain supreme amongst them. European navies and armed forces covered half the face of the world and they suppressed piracy because it was against their interests. No matter that these interests were sometimes dishonest such as the British support of the opium trade – piracy did not flourish for long. As the empires have dissolved, so too have the overseas navies and armed forces that supported them. One-time colonies and dependencies have become independent and, in many areas, trade has expanded, though in many cases this does not appear to have brought greatly increased standards of living to many. But flourishing trade brought more of the richer world's wealth within the poor nations' reach and many people subsidise themselves through robbery. The empires and forces which would once have combated piracy have long since gone. National forces in developing countries often depend on small budgets, and are inadequately equipped for dealing with crime. In Nigeria for example, the police rarely have finger printing equipment because they cannot afford it; when security passes were to be issued to the port staff in Lagos a few years ago, there was no money to buy the film to take their pictures.

So the richer world has gone in pursuit of wealth and in the course of trading with poorer nations many companies have experienced attacks on their shipping. In doing so a philosophy of non-interference and of expecting the world to be responsible for its own internal affairs has been adopted. But local security is often inadequate and although frequent complaints are made, in many cases the host nation just does not have the resources to improve the situation and should hardly be expected to put everything right overnight. Thus in many cases a choice must be made: to continue to suffer losses, to withdraw, or to insist on greater protection. Merchant ships should at least take greater steps to protect themselves, and it is abundantly apparent from the many reports in this book that often virtually no greater security measures are taken for protection overseas than in home ports.

As yet there does not appear to have been sufficient loss from ships to make the cost of providing greater protection worthwhile. The main damage has been to pride and to the sense of security and safety which those in command of major merchant ships expect, often having all their personal possessions around them. The major international organisation for dealing with such matters is the International Maritime Organisation of 127 nations – but at present it has no more than an advisory role and is in the process of organising a seminar on piracy – if it can find the money. Any move forward on this front is likely to be very slow.

The other types of piracy are more fundamental and cruel but they do not directly affect the world's merchant shipping. There would be no adverse effect on the economies of the developed world if every single one of the Vietnamese boat people were to be tortured, raped or murdered. Such awful incidents affect our consciences not our pockets and perhaps because of that we do very little about them.

The psychological effects of piracy are very real. It may not unduly trouble a shipowner that a safe containing several thousands of pounds has been stolen from one of his merchant ships but it will considerably disturb the master who has been tied up and beaten in the process and may continue to trouble him for years. We may not be particularly concerned by the fate of a 15-year-old Vietnamese girl passed from the hand of one fisherman to another in the Gulf of Siam but it will disturb her probably for the whole of her life. These attacks are matters of conscience and generally require minimal amounts of money to prevent. But what the attacks on merchant shipping also reveal is the ease with which anyone can get on board a large ship and take complete control of it. One day someone may wish to do so for greater purpose than to raid the safe. The majority of the world's cargo is transported by sea. Goods of every description are carried, from packets of cornflakes to nuclear bombs.

Here lies the problem for the future – some day someone will learn from these ignorant young men who are today's pirates just how easy the work is – they may go for much bigger pickings.

PART II
ATLAS OF PIRACY

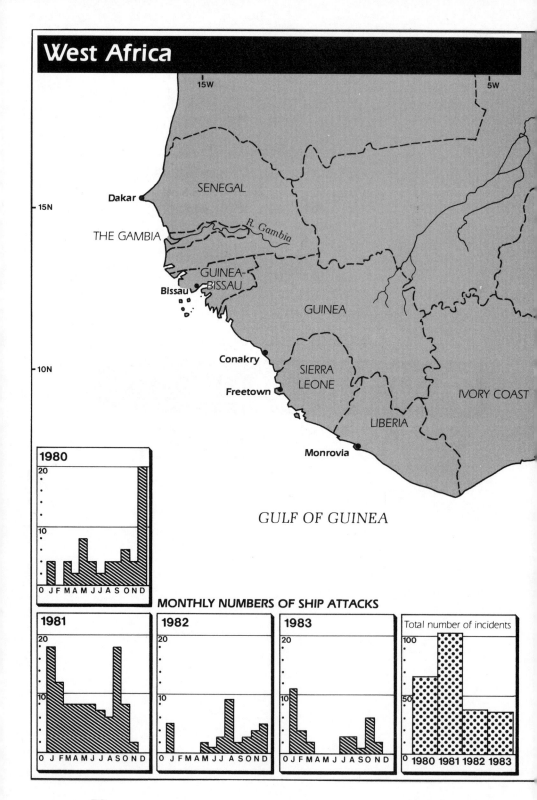

West Africa

15W

5W

15N

Dakar

SENEGAL

THE GAMBIA

R. Gambia

GUINEA-BISSAU

Bissau

GUINEA

10N

Conakry

SIERRA LEONE

Freetown

IVORY COAST

LIBERIA

Monrovia

GULF OF GUINEA

1980

20

10

0 J F M A M J J A S O N D

MONTHLY NUMBERS OF SHIP ATTACKS

1981

20

10

0 J F M A M J J A S O N D

1982

20

10

0 J F M A M J J A S O N D

1983

20

10

0 J F M A M J J A S O N D

Total number of incidents

100

50

0 1980 1981 1982 1983

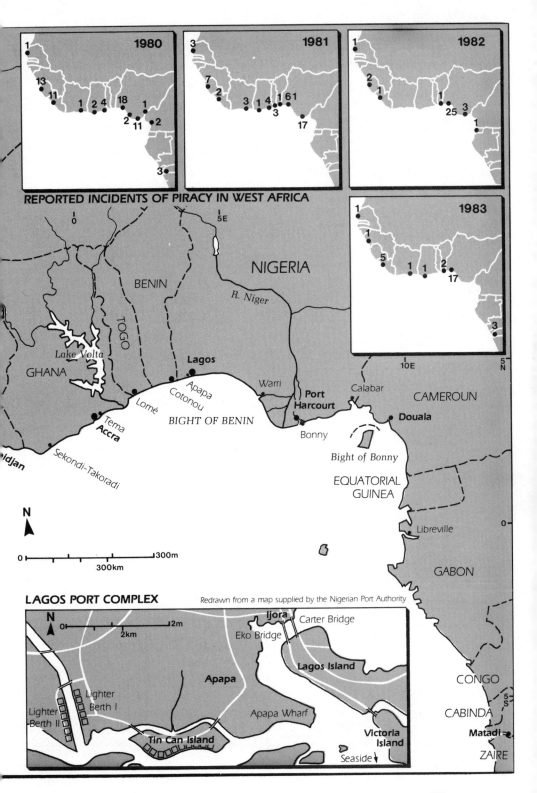

REPORTED INCIDENTS OF PIRACY IN WEST AFRICA

LAGOS PORT COMPLEX

Redrawn from a map supplied by the Nigerian Port Authority

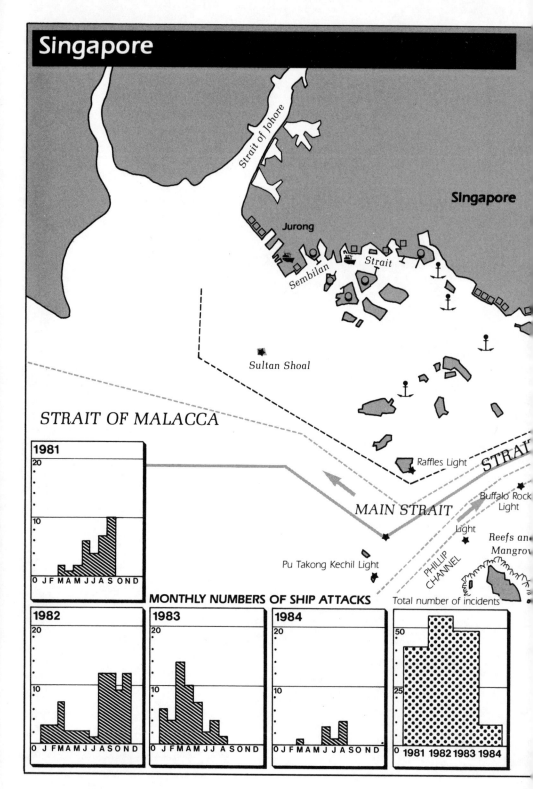

Singapore

Strait of Johore

Singapore

Jurong

Sembilan Strait

Strait

Sultan Shoal

STRAIT OF MALACCA

Raffles Light

STRAI

MAIN STRAIT

Buffalo Rock Light

Light

Reefs and Mangrov

Pu Takong Kechil Light

PHILLIP CHANNEL

1981

20

10

0 J F M A M J J A S O N D

MONTHLY NUMBERS OF SHIP ATTACKS

Total number of incidents

1982

20

10

0 J F M A M J J A S O N D

1983

20

10

0 J F M A M J J A S O N D

1984

20

10

0 J F M A M J J A S O N D

50

25

0 1981 1982 1983 1984

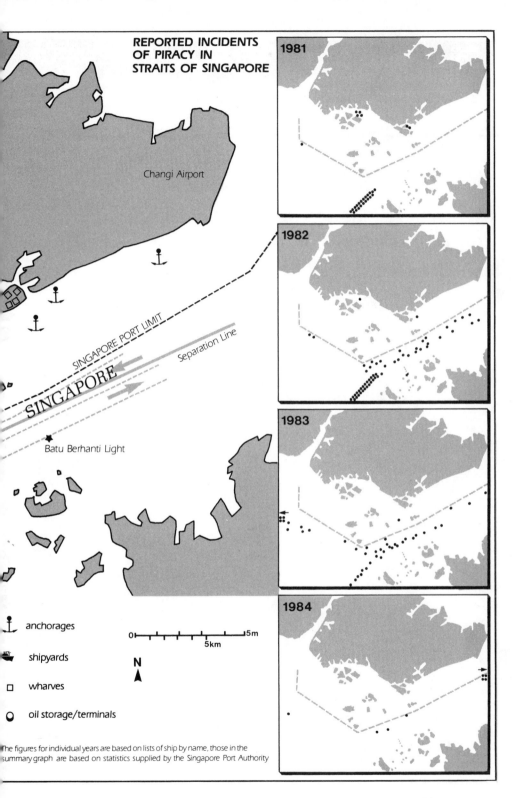

REPORTED INCIDENTS
OF PIRACY IN
STRAITS OF SINGAPORE

1981

1982

1983

1984

Changi Airport

SINGAPORE PORT LIMIT

Separation Line

SINGAPORE

Batu Berhanti Light

⚓ anchorages

🚢 shipyards

☐ wharves

○ oil storage/terminals

0 ├─┼─┼─┼─┼─┤ 5m
        5km

N
▲

The figures for individual years are based on lists of ship by name, those in the
summary graph are based on statistics supplied by the Singapore Port Authority

81

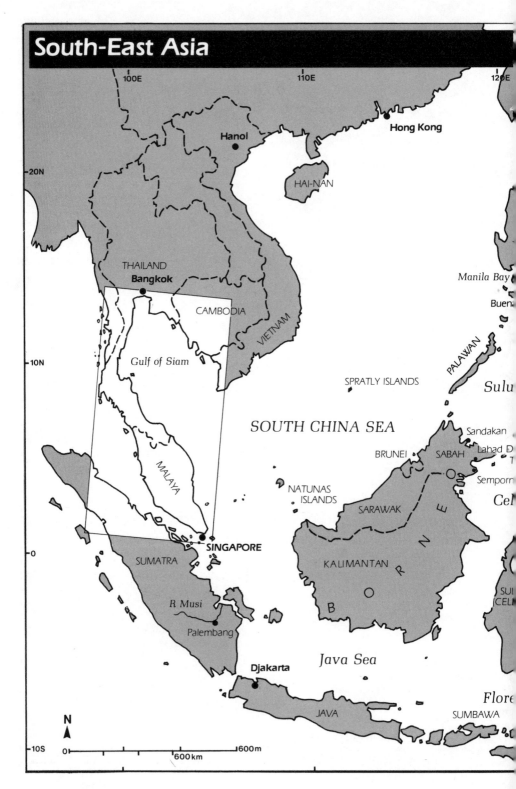

South-East Asia

100E
110E
120E

Hanoi
Hong Kong

20N

HAI-NAN

THAILAND
Bangkok
CAMBODIA
VIETNAM

Manila Bay
Buena

10N
Gulf of Siam
SPRATLY ISLANDS
Sulu

SOUTH CHINA SEA

Sandakan
BRUNEI
SABAH
Lahad D
T
Sempor
MALAYA
NATUNAS
ISLANDS
Cel

SARAWAK

R
N
E

SINGAPORE
KALIMANTAN

SUMATRA
O

SU
(CEL
B

R Musi
B

Palembang
Java Sea

Djakarta
Flore

JAVA
SUMBAWA

N

0
600m
600km

10S

82

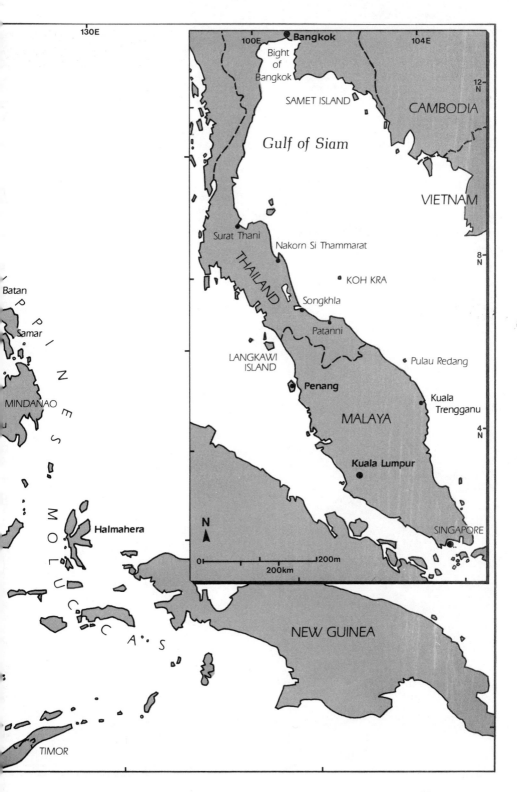

Batan

Samar

MINDANAO

Halmahera

TIMOR

130E

100E

Bangkok

Bight
of
Bangkok

SAMET ISLAND

Gulf of Siam

104E

12-N

CAMBODIA

VIETNAM

8-N

Surat Thani

Nakorn Si Thammarat

THAILAND

KOH KRA

Songkhla

Patanni

LANGKAWI
ISLAND

Penang

Pulau Redang

Kuala
Trengganu

4-N

MALAYA

Kuala Lumpur

SINGAPORE

N

0 ┃━━━━━━━━━━━━┃ 200m
        200km

NEW GUINEA

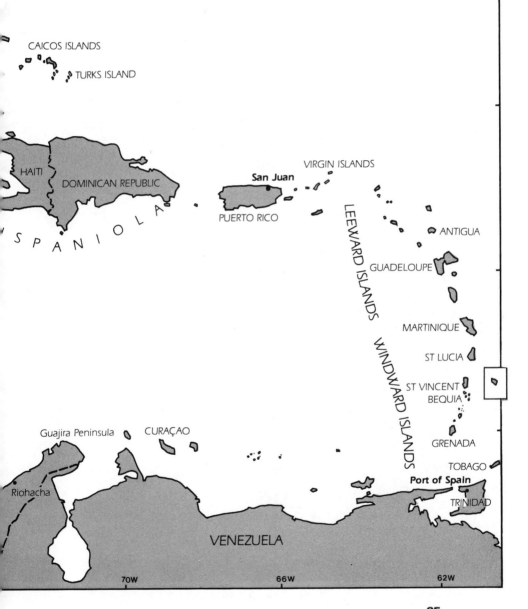

ATLANTIC OCEAN

CAICOS ISLANDS

TURKS ISLAND

HAITI

DOMINICAN REPUBLIC

VIRGIN ISLANDS

San Juan

PUERTO RICO

S P A N I O L A

LEEWARD ISLANDS

ANTIGUA

GUADELOUPE

MARTINIQUE

ST LUCIA

WINDWARD ISLANDS

ST VINCENT

BEQUIA

Guajira Peninsula

CURAÇAO

Riohacha

GRENADA

TOBAGO

Port of Spain

TRINIDAD

VENEZUELA

70W

66W

62W

N

CARIBBEAN SEA

HONDURAS

Puerto Cabezas

Gulf of Fonseca

NICARAGUA

COSTA RICA

PANAMA

GULF OF PANAMA

Barranquilla

Cartagena

Caracas

VENEZUELA

TOB

TRINIDAD

COLOMBIA

● **Bogota**

Buenaventura

PACIFIC OCEAN

Cabo San Lorenzo

● **Quito**

ECUADOR

Guayaquil

PERU

● **Lima**

PORT OF SANTOS

← Alemoa Jetty

Oil tanks

Wharves

Main Channel

Container terminal

Grain terminal

N

½m

0   1km

Bay of Santos

Yacht club

80W

70

CH

Part of Central and South America

orgetown
Paramaribo
Cayenne
ATLANTIC OCEAN
FRENCH
GUIANA
SURINAME
0
Sao Luís
Belém
Recife
10
S
BRAZIL
Salvador
20
S
OLIVIA
Sao Paulo
Rio de Janeiro
Santos
PARAGUAY
ARGENTINA
60W
50W
40W

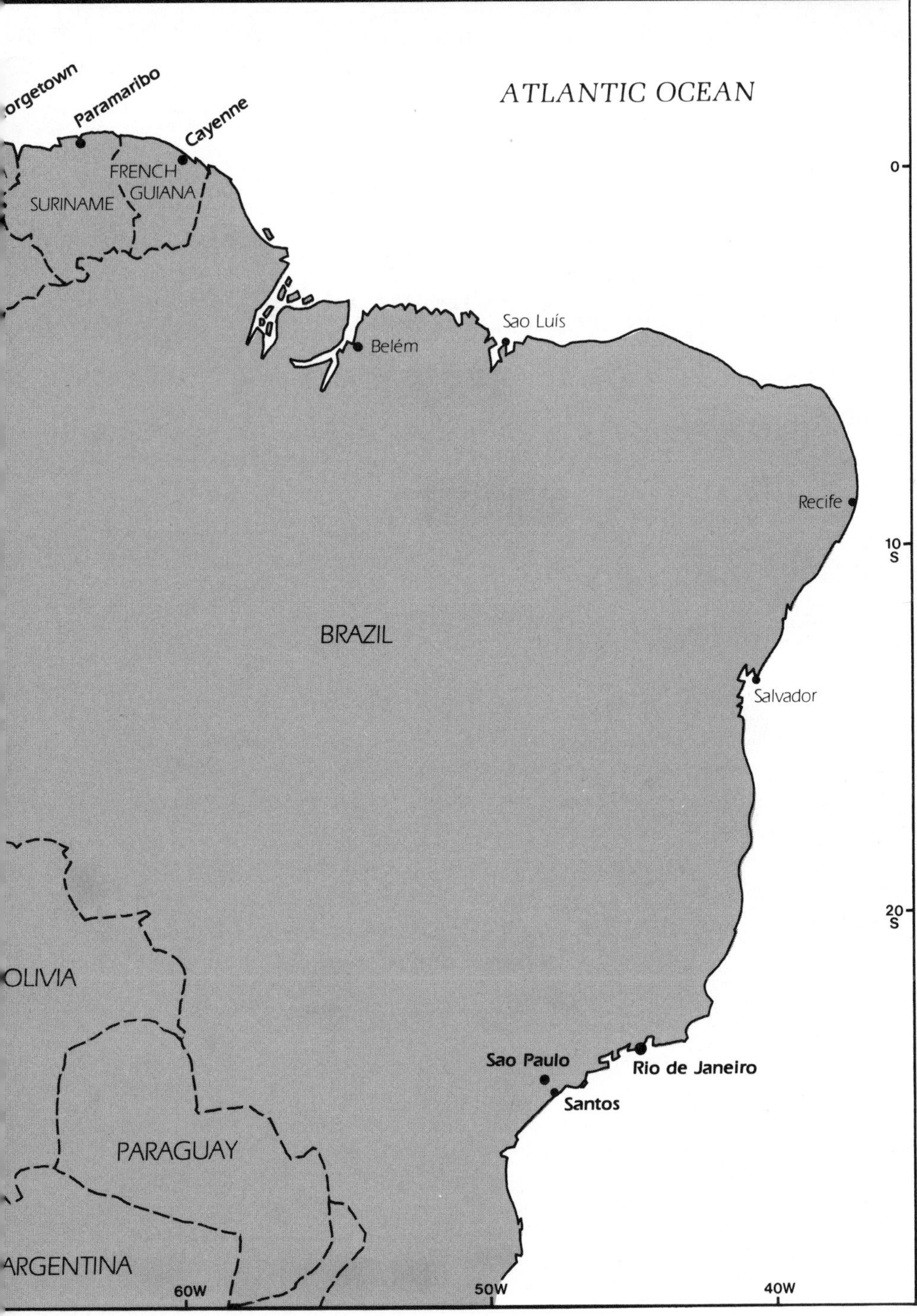

Terrorist black spots

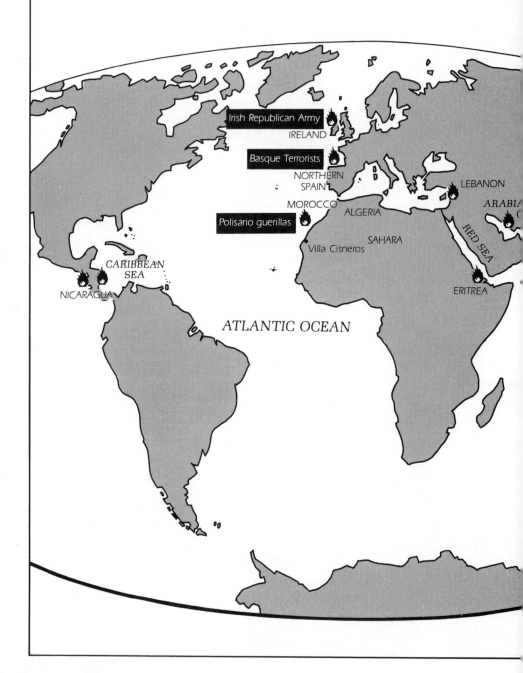

Irish Republican Army
IRELAND

Basque Terrorists
NORTHERN SPAIN

MOROCCO

Polisario guerillas

ALGERIA

LEBANON

ARABIA

RED SEA

SAHARA

Villa Cisneros

CARIBBEAN SEA

NICARAGUA

ERITREA

ATLANTIC OCEAN

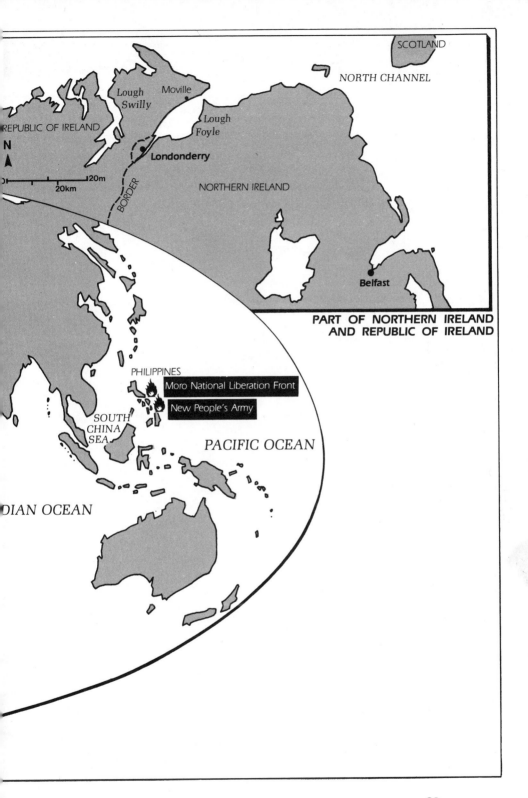

SCOTLAND

NORTH CHANNEL

Lough Swilly

Moville

REPUBLIC OF IRELAND

Lough Foyle

N

20m
20km

BORDER

Londonderry

NORTHERN IRELAND

Belfast

PART OF NORTHERN IRELAND
AND REPUBLIC OF IRELAND

PHILIPPINES

Moro National Liberation Front

New People's Army

SOUTH
CHINA
SEA

PACIFIC OCEAN

INDIAN OCEAN

PART III
LOG OF ATTACKS

The log of attacks contains the dates, locations, and brief particulars of all the incidents of piracy which it has been possible to trace between 1980 and 1984. (Excluding attacks on the Vietnamese boat people.) Prior to 1980 (1981 in Singapore) records were either not kept or have not been retained on file in sufficient numbers to make it worth their inclusion. The records for 1984 are probably incomplete at the time of writing but it is clear that attacks are still continuing in 1985. In certain cases the ship's name has been suppressed at the request of the owners.

It is the author's opinion that this is the most complete and comprehensive record in existence. Nevertheless, as has been explained in the text, it probably represents no more than about half of the actual number of attacks which have taken place.

Note: where details of ships' names, tonnage and registry are not included the facts were not available to the author or have been witheld at the request of the owners.

Reports of Piracy in the West African Area

The reports listed below do not include any attacks prior to 1980, nor do they include the numerous attacks on merchant shipping off the western Sahara, which on the whole seem to have been by Polisario guerillas.

• Map p78–9

26 January 1980 *Pitria*. Freetown. The gang employed in no 3 hatch broke into cases of cargo destined for ports other than Freetown. The chief officer was inspecting no 1 'tween deck when he found one case and 18 cartons for Abidjan were completely empty instead of containing T-shirts. At no 1 hatch, a case of cargo was carried to the side of the ship and thrown into the water and collected by a canoe. Later the chief officer found some labourers breaking into cartons of medicines for Tema in no 5 'tween deck and stealing the contents. Many cartons were found to have been pilfered. Security guards were present on the hatches throughout.

January 1980 British Ship. 12,091 tons. Apapa.
'There has been a renewed outbreak of piracy in Lagos Roads. ... On the same theme two junior officers' rooms were entered and burgled during the voyage, one whilst in Monrovia, the other in Lagos. Whilst alongside at Apapa the ship was boarded and a mooring rope cut ....'

January 1980 British ship. 13,447 tons. Tema. Master stated 'security in this port is poor although every effort was made to prevent pilferage. One gang was dismissed. In Ghana pharmaceuticals/medical preparations appear to be the prime target more so than foodstuffs.'

30 January 1980 British ship. 11,500 tons. Tema. Master stated 'pilferage was bad in Tema despite having security men in all hatches throughout discharge. Particularly vulnerable were foodstuffs, medicines, shoes, clothing and personal effects.'

March 1980 British ship. 11,961 tons. Takoradi. Three containers were broken into and the contents broached. The master advised 'it seems that the security and reliability of the stevedores being employed is very poor.'

7–8 March 1980 British ship. 13,447 tons. Dakar. Master reported 'During the course of discharge overnight ... the seals of 6 containers were removed by labour. The stevedores will not accept any liability as there is no "proof" that labour broke into the containers unless it is caught in the act'.

17 March 1980 Liberian ship. 12,091 tons. Apapa.
   'Earlier in the day at 1100 hours about 10 robbers boarded the ship and threw one carton (merchandise) and a roll of carpet into their fast boat, and in lightning mood they made away with the boat carrying their loot. A formal report was lodged to the Naval Base Apapa requesting for armed guard on board the vessel. A naval officer was on board by 1530 and after inspection he promised to send the armed guard which of course never turned up.'

31 March 1980 *Silver Arrow*. Greek registry. 16,658 tons. Freetown. Master reported
   'in no 2 hatch carton of shot-gun cartridges was discovered empty and the police at the dock gates later found persons leaving the ship with cartridges in their possession. These are part of a consignment for Warri stowed in the forepart of no 1 'tween deck. In no 4 'tween deck 8 cartons of electrical goods were found empty. Port security men were stationed in each of the above mentioned compartments but obviously were not very effective.'

21 April 1980 British ship. Freetown. Second officer caught stevedores lowering boxes of fine goods over the ship's side into waiting canoes from no 2 hatch. Several security guards were on duty at the time and they merely watched as this occurred. No attempt to stop the theft was made until the guards were reprimanded by the second officer. Six bales of material were stolen during the night from no 2 'tween deck which was closed after cargo operations.

April 1980 British ship. 14,067 tons. Freetown. Three containers were pilfered. The chief officer stated that the damage was done in Freetown after the lock on one of the trap hatches was broken off.

May 1980 British ship. 11,464 tons. West Africa. Master stated 'stealing in West Africa is just as bad and during the voyage at most ports we have had problems. I was ashore making an issue about it at Freetown.'

May 1980 British ship. 21,618 tons. Apapa.
'A steward was cleaning the bathroom in an officer's accommodation when he heard a noise in the cabin behind him. He looked out and discovered an intruder who he immediately tackled and called for help. Another steward and a ship's officer came to his assistance and the man was ultimately handed over to the police.'

1 May 1980 British ship. 21,618 tons. Apapa.
'During the daylight hours of Wednesday 30 April persons unknown cut and removed the onboard end of one of his vessel's mooring ropes.'

2 May 1980 British ship. 11,500 tons. Apapa. Master wrote
'I would like to draw your attention to the deplorable lack of any security that I have observed on the wharf. Gangs of thieves apparently at will roam up and down the wharf ready to loot cargo as soon as it is landed from the ship. Since commencement of discharge ... I have observed many instances of cargo being looted on the wharf. I observed thieves pulling open wooden packing cases to see what was inside. I observed a pallet of cartons containing chocolate bars being almost completely stolen by a gang of about ten thieves. Pallets of paper were pulled apart by thieves and their contents scattered over the wharf. I have made frequent complaints ... and for two hours one morning an armed guard was supplied. However, after eating on board at lunchtime, he then disappeared. The situation is completely intolerable.'

2 May 1980 British ship. Lagos.
'At 0340 the cadet disturbed 4–5 Africans who had burst the lock on a container containing household goods. The cadet alerted the other watchmen who called the crew while he called the deck officers. The vessel's siren was sounded and the request made on VHF to port operations for assistance but no reply received. The thieves made off in the meantime in a large canoe with an unknown quantity from the container.'

13 May 1980 British ship. 12,091 tons. Apapa. At 0330 boarded by approximately 15 men who opened 3 containers despite 6 security men and a ship's watchman on duty at the time. Vessel reported 'when spotted by the deck patrol the alarm was raised and in the ensuing fracas bottles were thrown at the watchman. The raiding party all managed to escape overside.'

14 May 1980 British ship. Douala. Master reported that stevedores were caught stealing pieces of cotton material by the ship's personnel but watchmen supplied from the shore did nothing to prevent these thefts.

20 May 1980 British ship. Matadi. A fridge container was opened and the contents broached.

24 May 1980 British ship. 15,000 tons. Las Palmas, Canary Islands. In early hours while waiting for the pilot prior to sailing, intruders were seen in vicinity of forward mast house on the port side. Four men were disturbed who promptly left by a rope into a boat moored alongside. Both locks on the port side forward mast house door and the trap hatch inside no 2 hatch had been forced and cargo in no 2 'tween deck had been moved. Reported by VHF to pilot station but no apparent effort made to contact police or to intercept the boat. Subsequently found that 24 cartons of cocoa butter had disappeared.

June 1980 British ship. 11,464 tons. Warri. Thirty metres of one of mooring ropes cut off on deck.

June 1980 British ship. 11,464 tons. Calabar. Master reported 'When we were in Calabar, which normally is a reasonably quiet place, we unfortunately, even with four watchmen being employed, lost a new tension wire from the forecastle head.'

2 June 1980 British ship. 11,464 tons. Freetown.
'Whilst the vessel was at anchor in Freetown harbour thieves boarded from a canoe and broke into a container …

They threw some cartons from the container into the water before being chased off the ship by the crew and security men. We also suspect that they threw some cartons of hazardous cargo into the water. They then picked up the cartons which had been thrown overboard and made off with them in their canoe. ... During the time the vessel has been in Freetown there has been a constant threat to the security of the cargo due to a lack of effective security in the port. Written complaints have been sent to the ship's agents by the master and the agents have taken up the matter with the port authority.'

10 June 1980 British ship. 11,464 tons. Master reported thefts of whisky from the lockers.

July 1980 British ship. 11,464 tons. Freetown.
'I regret to report that during the night-shift in Freetown the duty officers discovered four containers with broken seals. Some electrical goods were missing from one, some Ovaltine from another and the two remaining ones were still intact. At the same time the ship was being patrolled by six security guards but the officers found them dozing on occasions and a letter of complaint was given to the port authority.'

16 July 1980 British ship. 11,466 tons. Freetown. Containers of whisky, beer and batteries were broken into and some of the contents stolen.

22 July 1980 *Saint Paul.* French registry. 17,693 tons. Lagos. At 2330 boat and gang came alongside and forced and plunderd containers. Ship's officer on duty threatened with knife. Eight containers broached.

August 1980 British ship. Monrovia. Ten cartons of chloroquine tablets were landed empty but two thieves were apprehended at the gangway with small bottles of these medicines secreted on their person. The thieves were handed over to the military.

August 1980 British ship. 11,464 tons. Apapa.
'I regret to have to inform you that last night at 0015 the vessel was boarded by thieves who assaulted the second officer and one sailor while five containers were opened and the contents stolen ... He was able to see that there were two large canoes alongside the ship in which a large number of men were receiving boxes of cargo passed down to them

from a further group aboard the ship . . . some of the gang had been hiding near to his [the officer's] position and on his shouting they leaped out and grabbed him. During the course of the ensuing scuffle the second officer received two bad bites, one on the right shoulder and one in the centre of his back. Whilst one man was doing the biting, another was hitting him on the head with a piece of wood. In addition to the cargo stolen, the second officer lost his watch and his uniform almost torn from his back is now beyond repair.'

August 1980 British ship. 15,381 tons. Freetown.
'We had 400 cartons of whisky for Freetown and some whisky for Douala stowed in the same compartment. As discharging was continuing the situation got more and more out of hand, as the labourers were getting drunk and the police, security, and customs officers were only interested in getting their share of the loot. As we, the ship, can get no help from the port authority in these matters, we are more or less helpless in trying to prevent damage and stealing of the cargo.'

16 August 1980 British ship. 11,617 tons. Freetown.
'It appears that stevedores down the hatch are continuously broaching cargo, even though security guards down the hatch seem ample. Thieves forced open a locked clothes locker in the greasers' alleyway stealing several items of clothing. Stevedores appear to carry off the ship small packages in front of security guards with very little action taken. Organised thieves seem to board every vessel that is in port.'
The chief officer advised that six containers were opened and part of the contents pilfered.

September 1980 British ship. 11,500 tons. Apapa. Lock to hatch no 3 forced and radios stolen from three Mercedes cars.
'Thieving and violence is unfortunately on the increase in Apapa and the port area. Vessels are being boarded from both the lagoon and wharf sides by gangs of up to 30 men, usually the first night the vessel berths. The authorities seem unable or unwilling to do anything about it.'

September 1980 British ship. 12,091 tons. Freetown. Thieves gained access to six containers stowed on deck. The master states that pilfering 'has reached epidemic proportions at Freetown from deck and hold cargo.'

6 September 1980 British ship. Matadi. 'An upsurge of pilferage in this port. During the night of 6 September thieves broke into a container for Pointe Noire and stole six cartons of whisky.'

8–22 September 1980 *Nedlloyd Madras.* Netherlands registry. 17,525 tons. Apapa. Boarded by armed thieves on nine occasions up to 22 September.

October 1980 British ship. 11,617 tons. Freetown. Pilfering was so extensive that the master telephoned the owners from Freetown to advise what was going on. Apart from the other incidents mentioned, the chief officer found an intruder in the saloon with his pockets full of the ship's cutlery. Moreover thieves were found in the lower hold with lighted torches to assist them in finding the best cargo to pilfer.

9 October 1980 British ship. 11,618 tons. Freetown. Thieves broke into a container and stole part of the contents. The chief officer of the vessel also reported '... the hatch security men appear to work in collaboration with those thieving.'

19 October 1980 British ship. 21,618 tons. Apapa. Thieves boarded at anchor and broke seals on five containers. Chased off by patrolling crew and officers.

20 October 1980 British ship. 11,617 tons. Freetown. On the upper deck 12 containers were broken into during the night despite a security force of 9 men which included 2 policemen, one of whom was armed. The master stated

> 'I can only assume the thieves got on board and put pressure on the nine watchmen to keep quiet ... this incident is a repeat of an incident last voyage ... I understand that other vessels calling here are having the same problem and this thieving goes on continuously. It would appear that this thieving is organised ... as it is always the most broachable containers that lose the most. I have had reports that thieves have threatened action against the families of watchmen etc, so this would limit a watchman's actions.'

25 October 1980 British ship. 21,618 tons. Apapa. Ten men boarded with axes and attempted theft from a container. Ship's officers arrived and thieves left after throwing stones. Security supervisor had axe held at throat.

26 October 1980 British ship. 21,618 tons. Apapa. Chief officer attacked from quay near gangway by four men who stole watch. Numerous people about but no help.

November 1980 British ship. 11,464 tons. Freetown. Similar report on the use of lighted torches to that on another British ship of 11,617 tons in October 1980.

7 November 1980 British ship. 11,464 tons. Douala. Pilot advised master that on the previous night 40–50 persons had boarded another ship from four large canoes and smashed their way into containers stowed on board. The master also stated that in respect of his own vessel 'we only worked until 2200 hours at night and that with heavy lifts only because there is no way that the labour can be controlled after that time as they just openly steal the cargo.'

22 November 1980 British ship. 12,091 tons. Tema. Two containers were broken open by shore labour. The master also stated in his deck logbook '... due to indiscriminate and uncontrolled pilfering by shore labour all cargo operations had to be suspended.'

27 November 1980 British ship. 11,464 tons. Freetown.
'The ship berthed at 0810 hours and after clearance hordes of people boarded the ship, gangway labourers, agency watchmen, port security guards, friends of the African crew members and amongst these people a number of thieves gained access to the accommodation, no restriction by the guards at the gangway being imposed. Two thieves were caught in possession of the officer's lounge cassette equipment. Discharge commenced at 1000 hours and for the following 3½ days incidents of thieving to cargo took place during discharge despite attempts by ship's staff to prevent thefts without becoming physically involved.'
The master goes on to detail the losses from vehicles, wire lashings, general cargo, containers, deck cargo, etc. He further states that thefts took place without the guards taking any action.

December 1980 British ship. 11,961 tons. Matadi. Labourers deliberately smashed open the top of the container to gain access to the contents. When the container was opened 8 cartons of whisky were found to be broached with a total loss of 96 bottles.

3 December 1980 British ship. 12,091 tons. Bonny. Boarded in early hours by about 15 men from three canoes. 'Apparently the pirates have their own VHF as we heard on our own VHF a reply to a call from Bonny "This is ... [repeating ship's name]. Our crew now on deck." No shore assistance given whatever.'

4–5 December 1980 *St Paul*. French registry. 17,693 tons. Lagos. At least 12 pirates on board at about 0200 with machetes and axes. Broached five containers in about half an hour.

5 December 1980 Liberian ship. 19,607 tons. Abidjan. At 0430 while anchoring in inner harbour and awaiting berth, the duty quartermaster and two local watchmen were found tied up with rope in no 1 hold and some of the cargo containers were opened and pilfered. On 6 December at about 0530, while alongside the wharf, the duty officer gave continuous long blast on siren as he found about 20 armed robbers climbing up the ship's side and intending to rob again. They ran away immediately when chased by crew with fire-axes, crowbars, pipes, etc.

8 December 1980 *Pitria*. Tema. 'There were 21 bales of textiles stowed in no 4 'tween deck and at Tema on the morning of 8 February the chief officer opened the no 4 hatch and noticed that some of the bales were missing which had been in good order and condition when the hatch was locked on the previous night. Ship's officers with two policemen searched the hatch and many pieces of cloth were discovered in the lower hold – some hidden under vehicles and others inside the boots of cars. The discrepancies were quite heavy.'

10 December 1980 *Johnny Wesch*. West German registry. 4525 tons. Apapa. Boarded on five occasions while alongside quays. On one occasion the crew were threatened with knives.
'The way of a raid is always the same. Thieves get among the stevedores and as soon as their boats are alongside they quickly fill up the boats with some handy cargo either out of containers or out of the hatches.'

14 December 1980 Italian ship. 3096 tons. Dawes Island. At 0100 reported on VHF being boarded by marauders.

16 December 1980 *Nedlloyd Manila*. Dutch registry. 17,525 tons. Apapa. Anchored eight miles from shore. Five men boarded at the bow and opened containers on no 1 hatch which were empty and went down to holds nos 2 and 3. Tried to open them but did not succeed so they left the ship.

16 December 1980 Greek ship. Bonny Fairway Anchorage. Boarded by some 20 marauders who broke into containers on deck. No details.

19 December 1980 Cypriot ship. 7554 tons. Bonny. Boarded in early hours.

19 December 1980 *Saint Jacques*. French registry. Bonny. Boarded in early hours by 75 men.

22 December 1980 *United Bounty*. Liberian registry. 14,488 tons. Bonny Fairway Anchorage. Boarded at 0200 by marauders from six to eight boats.

24 December 1980 *Andrea Smits*. Dutch registry. 6110 tons. Boarded at Dockyard Creek, Bonny by 40–50 marauders. Ship called four times for assistance. At 0345 vessel was again boarded and further damage was done to containers on deck No response from authorities.

27 December 1980 *Tey Kaiser*. Japanese registry. 10,212 tons. Bonny. Boarded by 40–50 marauders. Four containers broached.

27 December 1980 British ship. 21,618 tons. Apapa. Ship's lockers broken into and rope slings stolen.

31 December 1980 West German ship. 13,879 tons. Lagos/Port Harcourt. No details available.

31 December 1980 British ship. 11,610 tons. Bonny. Boarded by some 20–30 marauders. Bonny signals called on VHF but ship was only advised to lift gangway and told that it was too early to call the police.

31 December 1980 British ship. 11,464 tons. Warri. Labour broke into container of whisky for Douala and approximately 12 cases stolen and consumed by the labourers who became aggressive and intoxicated during this time.

31 December 1980 British ship. Takoradi. 74 bales of cotton piece goods for Matadi were pilfered in no 2 lower hold. Also observed thieves broaching cases on the rail car on the wharf and the police merely looking on taking no action. Thieving more prevalent on this voyage in spite of vigilance of ship's officers. Numerous police on vessel and the wharf did nothing to stop this obvious pilferage. Gangway men and port security men did nothing to prevent large sacks of cargo going down the gangway. Ship's officers were taking retrieved cargo to the shed for checking and part of this was confiscated by border guards. The cargo was not returned to the vessel prior to departure. Two containers for Matadi were broached. Two cases for Abidjan were found at Takoradi, having been overstowed but they disappeared and the master could only assume that they were stolen at Takoradi.

31 December 1980 *Nigerian Brewer*. West German registry. 7550 tons. Port Harcourt, at no 5 buoy in Dockyard Creek discharging into barges (four alongside). At 0700 in full daylight 12 big canoes, each with 5-6 men, approached from the north. All were power driven by fast outboard-type twin motors. Four came to port side and cut one barge's mooring ropes which then drifted astern on the one remaining mooring wire. Suddenly two boats approached and gave orders and they all moved off, possibly because other traffic was using the river. When this traffic cleared, they came back and tried to release the barge but may have noticed that containers were then empty. All then moved off. Nothing stolen. Shore alerted by VHF channel 16. Two Nigerian policemen on board throughout but not seen during this time. The attack was very well organized and carried out in a strategic manner.

In early 1981 it was reported that up to twelve ocean-going vessels were being attacked daily at Apapa and Lagos. Not all of these will be included in the lists below.

1981 (exact date unknown) *Saint Paul*. French registry. 17,693 tons. Cotonou Roads. Attacked by about a dozen pirates armed with machetes.

1981 (exact date unknown) British ship. 3384 tons. Lagos. Pirated alongside and second officer held at knife-point. But pirates were after no more than paint.

1981 (exact date unknown) Liberian ship. 4634 tons. Lagos. No details available.

1 January 1981 British ship. 11,617 tons. Freetown. Two containers pilfered. A Bedford lorry stowed on deck had one side window, one battery and one tool kit stolen.

2 January 1981 Liberian ship. 19,607 tons. Dockyard Creek, Bonny. Boarded by 12 marauders who were chased off.

4 January 1981 *Globe Trader.* Singapore registry. 8094 tons. Bonny. Boarded by marauders from ten boats at 0100. Message overheard on VHF that two boats were arrested by Bonny pilot boat and police.

4–5 January 1981 Japanese container ship. 60–80 marauders boarded at Bonny anchorage and pilfered deck containers.

5 January 1981 Unknown. Bonny. Reported boarded by 60–80 marauders at the fairway buoy.

5 January 1981 West German ship. 13,879-ton container vessel. Lagos/Port Harcourt. Numerous attacks reported with foodstuffs, oil, and autoparts stolen.

6 January 1981 *Esmeralda 1.* Bonny Anchorage. Heavily attacked by marauders.

7 January 1981 British ship. 11,618-ton general cargo ship. Port Harcourt.
   'Boarded by 15 armed robbers who broached 9 containers and stole an estimated total of 2 tonnes of cargo. Two Krooboy watchmen were slightly injured and no assistance was received during the raid from authorities ashore.'

7 January 1981 *British ship.* 11,484 tons. Port Harcourt. Master noted ten instances of other vessels boarded by thieves. These have been included in this overall list.

7 January 1981 *Usambara.* Lagos. No details available.

12 January 1981 *Togo Brewer.* West German registry. 7550 tons. Lagos/Port Harcourt. No details available.

15 January 1981 British ship. 13,447 tons. Takoradi.
   'On routine inspection of the explosives compartment in no 5 hatch at 0630 hours this morning, the third officer noted that the padlock was found to be broken off and the locker had been forced open. The contents of the locker were then shifted and check tallied into a container. A total of 120 cartons had been manifested and the check showed a shortage of 29 cartons and 27 empty.'

18 January 1981 British ship. 18,863 tons. Bonny. No details available.

February 1981 *Pep Sea*. Danish registry. 1385 tons. Lagos. No details available.

February 1981 *Korsten Wesch*. West German registry. Lagos. Secured to buoys and not working cargo. During night pirates cut the after mooring ropes to buoy and vessel swung to tide and hit pier on Lagos Esplanade. During this confusion, pirates raided containers.

5 February 1981 *Britta Oden*. Swedish registry. 6950 tons. Lagos. No details available.

7 February 1981 British ship. 18,863 tons. Lagos. No details available.

7 February 1981 *Lisbet Coast*. Lagos. No details available

12 February 1981 *British Tenacity*. British registry. 24,227-ton tanker. Lagos. At anchor nine miles WSW of Lagos Breakwater Head waiting to berth and discharge cargo. In morning pirates boarded and broke open lock of forecastle door to get access to ships store rooms. All hands on deck at 0350. Pirates jumped over side without stealing anything. General warning broadcast but no patrol boat sent out.

12 February 1981 *Remco*. Ghanaian registry. 2627 tons. Lagos. Attacked and crew injured by pirates who stole some of their personal belongings.

19 February 1981 *Opal Bounty*. Liberian registry. 6583 tons. Off Lagos. Arrived in anchorage at 0715 and boarded by pirates shortly after in three boats with some 30 men. Crew tried to repel them but suffered minor injuries. Three containers opened and part of contents stolen. Vessel steamed out of anchorage dragging anchor. Pirates eventually left.

18–21 February 1981 *Urundi*. West German registry. Lagos/Port Harcourt. No details available.

20 February 1981 *Baco Liner*. West German registry. 22,000-ton barge container-carrying ship. Lagos/Port Harcourt. No details available.

24 February 1981 *Pep Sea*. Danish registry. 1385 tons. Lagos. No details available.

24 February 1981 *Chai Varee*. Thai registry. 18,632 tons. Lagos. No details available.

21 March 1981 *La Falda.* British registry. 3384 tons. Apapa. No details available.

26 March 1981 *Seevetal.* West German registry. 7679 tons. Lagos. No details available.

28 March 1981 *Seevetal.* West German registry. 7679 tons. At 0225 reported 'Vessel being attacked and pirates still on board. Anchored 5.5 miles from breakwater.'

28 March 1981 *Grete Sif.* Danish registry. 1941 tons. Lagos. No details available.

29 (?) March 1981 *Nedlloyd Manila.* Dutch registry. 17,525 tons. Lagos. Overnight pirates boarded, held up second officer, and removed about 20 bales of rags (which are suits in Nigeria).

9 March 1981 British ship. British registry. 12,726 tons. Lagos. No details available.

30 March 1981 Unknown Yugoslav. Lagos. Reported two boats had come with pirates. No reply from port commandant on VHF.

31 March 1981 *Westwall.* Dutch registry. 2970 tons. Lagos. Reported pirates on board at 0448. No reply on VHF from East Mole or port commandant.

1 April 1981 *Riverina.* British registry. 9127 tons. Lagos. At Marine buoys. At 0630 saw two boats approaching with five men. Went to lighter alongside and threw some 25 bags of cement into each boat before making off down harbour. Too far for hose jets to be used.

15 April 1981 *Tarubi.* Cypriot registry. 6685 tons. Lagos. No details available.

18 April 1981 *Baucis.* Cypriot registry. 6126 tons. Lagos/Port Harcourt. No details available.

19 April 1981 *Anangel Luck.* Greek registry. 15,673 tons. Lagos. No details available.

19 April 1981 *Yin Kim.* Panama registry. 24,845 tons. Lagos. No details available.

20 April 1981 Name unknown. Polish registry. Lagos. No details available.

21 April 1981 *Northridge.* British registry. 3440 tons. Lagos. No details available.

22 April 1981 *Mount King.* Panama registry. 6750 tons. Lagos. No details available.

16 May 1981 *Balticland.* Swedish registry. 10,899 tons. Abidjan. Shifting to no 19/20 berth on quay and moored at 1250. The mooring deck was stormed by 10–15 persons who broke open containers of auto-tyres which they threw to others on the quay. Three watchmen and crew chased them away. A single policeman arrived at 1700. Roughly 50 tyres stolen.

18 May 1981 *Balticland.* Swedish registry. 10,899 tons. Abidjan. At no 22 berth. At 0545 alarm raised that ship being invaded by thieves. At least 50 had climbed on board and were throwing tyres ashore. They were armed with knives and threw large stones at the crew. Left about 0630 after having stolen some 150 tyres.

25 May 1981 *Balticland.* Swedish registry. 10,899 tons. Lagos. Anchored in Lagos Roads. At 2335 found boat secured to port chain cable and men entering forecastle where they opened containers. VHF used to ask for help but none came. Main engine put slow ahead and rudder hard to starboard. Screams heard from boat. Pirates departed. Some containers damaged but nothing stolen. During the night several ships reported pirates on VHF but no assistance given from the shore.

22 May 1981 *Nedlloyd Niger.* Dutch registry. 12,403 tons. Lagos. Anchored eight miles south of breakwater on 21st. On 22nd small boat seen approaching on radar at about 0400 close to port bow. *Nedlloyd Niger* sounded siren, switched on deck lights, and sprayed water from deck hoses. All ships warned. Small boat had powerful outboard engine and kept alongside and started to throw bottles at sailor on duty. Threw grappling hook on board and one coloured man climbed in but, when he saw so many crew close to, he retreated back into his boat which cast off though they still threw bottles. Came back again at 0455 and while ship was ready to heave anchor, she was bombarded with bottles. Ship moved off at 0514. No apparent damage or theft.

22 May 1981 *Moolchand.* Lagos. About 0400 boarded by eight pirates who were armed with guns, breaking open the containers, and moving towards the quarters. Other ships took up plea for help and continuous messages went to the authorities. No answer came. Called mayday at 0715 on VHF channel 16 but no answer. At 0814 heard that help was coming and at 0830 told to 'have no fear' as a navy vessel was underway. *Moolchand* answered that pirates had just left.

23 May 1981 Name unknown. French registry. Lagos. No details available.

23 May 1981 *Nedlloyd Schelde*. Dutch registry. 12,904 tons. Lagos. No details available.

28 May 1981 Trader ship. Lagos. No details available.

1 June 1981 *Eva*. Greek registry. 7628 tons. Lagos. No details available.

1 June 1981 *Uta-Sabine*. West German registry. 7500 tons. Lagos/Port Harcourt. No details available.

7–13 June 1981 *Chai Varee*. Thai registry. 18,632 tons. Apapa. No details available.

11–15 June 1981 *Rafaela*. Panama registry. 6152 tons. Lagos. Anchored in Lagos roads 4½ miles from port entrance. First attack at midnight on 11th when ten men in boat approached and tried to get on board with grappling hooks. Repelled but shouted that they would return and kill everyone on board. Reported to port authorities whose advice was to leave the area. On 14th at 2200 three boats attacked and 40 men armed with knives tried for two hours to get on board. Port authorities were informed and told master 'no berthing instructions.' On 15th three big motor boats with many people approached and there were considerable problems in repelling the attack. Pirates attempted to climb through anchor chain pipe but crew sealed it off. Attack was all round ship and master succeeded in repelling only when he started to manoeuvre with the main engine.

13 June 1981 Name unknown. Lagos. No details available.

15 June 1981 *Ocean Eminence*. Liberian registry. 18,627 tons. Lagos. No details available.

18 June 1981 *Canis Major*. Panama registry. 11,711 tons. Lagos. No details available.

20–30 June 1981 *Stintfang*. West German registry. 8150 tons. Lagos/Port Harcourt. No details available.

14–17 July 1981 Two British ships. 11,618 and 14,067 tons. Lagos and Port Harcourt. 'Lying off awaiting berths. Preservation of law and order not a strong feature of life in Nigeria at that time'. No details.

5 July 1981 *Pia Danielsen*. Danish registry. 21,300 tons. Lagos. Pirates armed with crowbars, knives, and bottles stole bales of stockfish.

18 July 1981 British ship. 14,067 tons. Lagos. No details available.

24 July 1981 *Margrethe Maersk*. Danish registry. 21,300 tons. Lagos. Men's jogging shoes stolen from cargo. No other details available.

25 July 1981 *Blue Akeishi*. Japanese registry. 7058 tons. Lagos. No details available.

28 July 1981 Danish ship. 19,149 tons. Monrovia. No details available.

29 July 1981 Name Unknown. Greek registry. Apapa. No details available.

August 1981 Name Unknown. Port Harcourt. While alongside, pirates tried to board at 0400 and to open containers on deck. Prevented by ship's crew and eventually the police arrived.

10 August 1981 Name Unknown. Apapa. No details available.

27 August 1981 *Nedlloyd Nile*. Dutch registry. 12,403 tons. Tema. Discharging cargo at 0730 employing five gangs. Uncontrollable pilferage especially from cartons of medicines and of Schick razors.

29 August 1981 British ship. 21,618 tons. Lagos. No details available.

30 August 1981 *Nedlloyd Nile*. Dutch registry. 12,403 tons. Lome. Berthed at 0720. Much pilferage of handbags, tinned chickens, tinned milk and sugar.

30 August 1981 *Sloman Merkur*. West German registry. 13,500 tons. Lagos/Port Harcourt. No details available.

September 1981 *Rafaela.* Panama registry. 10,200 ton general cargo ship. Apapa/Lagos. No details available.

September 1981 *Africa Maru.* Japanese registry. 18,685 tons. Apapa/Lagos. No details available.

September 1981 *Chai Varee.* Thai registry. 18,632 tons. Apapa/Lagos. No details available.

September 1981 *Tendai Maru.* Japanese registry. 18,000 ton bulk carrier. Apapa/Lagos. No details available.

September 1981 *Pia Danielsen.* Danish registry. 2350-ton general cargo ship. Apapa/Lagos. Attacked by pirates who stole bales of stockfish.

September 1981 *Atlantic Maru.* Japanese registry. 18,600 tons. Apapa/Lagos. Attacked by pirates who took contents of a container.

September 1981 *Nedlloyd Fresco.* Dutch registry. 12,335 tons. Apapa. Numerous watchmen, including 'bow and arrow' men employed, but excessive pilferage was experienced.

2 September 1981 *Nedlloyd Niger.* Dutch registry. 12,403 tons. Apapa (Tin Can Island). Five watchmen on board from shore and four 'bow and arrow' men patrolling deck during the dark hours. About 0700 the third officer was threatened by thieves armed with knives. Alarm raised and thieves fled in a canoe with outboard motor. Locks forced on two containers on deck.

September 1981 *Nedlloyd Fresco.* Dutch registry. 12,335 tons. Lome. No local watchmen could be engaged and heavy pilferage from cargo. Requested police' protection in vain.

8 September 1981 British Ship. 12,091 tons. Monrovia. No details available.

9 September 1981 *Nedlloyd Fresco.* Dutch registry. 12,335 tons. Tema. At 0130 while anchored in outer roads, attacked by ten armed bandits who tied up and threatened the duty officer and broke into hold no 4 and stole textiles, one lift-van, cassette recorders, four guy ropes, and watch from duty officer. Very heavy pilferage in the port.

11(?) November 1981 *Nedlloyd Fresco.* Dutch registry. 12,335 tons. Dakar. Watchmen, custom guards, and police could not stop excessive pilferage of cargo both on board and on the wharf.

15–17 September 1981 *Taifun*. West German registry. 7554-ton general cargo ship. Apapa/Lagos. Attacked three times by pirates who stole boxes and injured master.

25 September 1981 *Nedlloyd Manila*. Dutch registry. 17,525 tons. Abidjan. Despite constant supervision, some containers opened and contents stolen.

27 September 1981 *New Panda*. Panama registry. 15,079 tons. Lagos Roads. Attacked by pirates but no details.

28 September 1981 *Nedlloyd Manila*. Dutch registry. 17,525 tons. Apapa. Seven pirates in speedboat attacked at 0715 and broke open a container and stole about 25 cartons.

October 1981 *Portoseuta*. 45 miles off Mauretania. Fishing vessel boarded by three pirates from rubber motor boat who shot four fishermen, killing one of them.

3 October 1981 *Polana*. Greek registry. Dakar. No details available.

5 October 1981 *Nedlloyd Manila*. Dutch registry. 17,525 tons. Lome. One container found broken open.

7–8 October 1981 *Nedlloyd Manila*. Dutch registry. 17,525 tons. Tema. Four containers found broken open and pilfered.

9 October 1981 *Paean*. Greek registry. 5318 tons. Apapa/Lagos. Attacked by pirates who stole bags of cement.

28 October 1981 *Nedlloyd Marseilles*. Dutch registry. 17,525 tons. Apapa. About 0330 at Berth A17A, raided by 10 to 15 pirates who broached and pilfered 2 containers. Boarded unobserved from small craft somewhere forward. Two crew members on deck patrol were ambushed and held at knife-point and threatened with death if they tried to escape. Nevertheless they ran off and sounded the alarm. The pirates driven off and police arrived in a few minutes. Were not after valuable containers so apparently had no pre-knowledge of contents.

28 October 1981 *Esk*. Dakar. No details available.

30(?) October 1981 *Nedlloyd Marseilles*. Dutch registry. 17,525 tons. Tema. Despite vigorous and continued efforts, unknown persons boarded and tampered with containers when being handled. Some contents stolen.

November 1981 Name unknown. Dawes Island at anchor. Two small fast canoes circled ship at 0200 and disappeared. Came back at 0430 with reinforcements and tried to board but were prevented by the crew.

4 November 1981 *Amaranta.* Portuguese registry. 14,438 tons. Lagos/Port Harcourt. No details available.

1982 (exact date unknown) *Lucky Penny.* Cypriot registry. 9718 tons. Lagos at anchor. No details available.

1982 (exact date unknown) *Southwind.* Alongside at Lagos. No details available.

January 1982 Name unknown. Bonny Roads. In the anchorage four miles south of the fairway buoy and 15 miles from land. After an initial reconnaissance, two very large cargo canoes with about 35 men all told, attacked at 0430. As they approached, they started hurling beer bottles and other missiles on to the main deck but also used small explosive charges (detonators) whose blast was sufficient to blow a hole in one of the fire hoses being used to fend off the boats. The pirates appeared partially drunk. Fortunately there were no casualties among the crew.

January 1982 *Vegaland.* Equatorial Guinea. Attacked but no details available.

28 January 1982 *Nedlloyd Marseilles.* Dutch registry. 17,525 tons. Apapa. Alongside at berth A17A. At 0310 raided by 15 pirates from two fast speedboats despite deck patrol and 'bow and arrow' men. Raiders driven off with assistance of police but some pilfering found.

7 February 1982 British ship. 11,618 tons. Freetown. No details available.

11–13 April 1982 Name unknown. West German registry. Apapa. No details available.

30–31 April 1982 British ship. 11,618 tons. No details available.

26 June 1982 *Nordheide.* West German registry. 7350 tons. Lagos. No details available.

July 1982 *Frigo Asia.* Spanish registry. 4462 tons. Off Apapa/Lagos waiting to berth. Attacked at 0200 by six pirates who overpowered crew and stole $8,000 and some valuables.

July 1982 *Kirsten Frank.* Off Apapa/Lagos. General cargo ship. Pirates stole fish.

July 1982 *Arlil.* Off Apapa/Lagos. 700-ton general cargo ship. Pirates stole unspecified valuables.

3 August 1982 *African Camellia.* USA registry. 8992 tons. Lagos, at anchor in Harbour pool. Four pirates with pistol and knife rob master.

5 August 1982 *White Star.* Panama registry. 12,697-ton general cargo ship. Lagos. No details available.

August 1982 *Nedlloyd Steenkerk.* Dutch registry. 12,256 tons. Lagos. 12,256-ton general cargo ship. Three crew members wounded (relatively minor) by pirates who boarded ship. Message to raise harbour authorities and to get a doctor failed. Attacked twice in all.

12 August 1982 *Antares.* Apapa/Lagos. Pirates damaged accommodation and stole various articles.

13 August 1982 *African Hyacinth.* Lagos. Boarded by four pirates in the early morning.

17 August 1982 *Seki Rolette.* Japanese registry. Monrovia. Cargo ship. No details available.

22 August 1982 *Nedlloyd Steenkirk.* Dutch registry. 12,256 tons. Lagos. No details available.

24 August 1982 *Seki Rolette.* Japanese registry. Lagos. No details available.

29 August 1982 *Pampero.* West German registry. 7434-ton general cargo ship. Apapa. No details available.

6–10 September 1982 Three ships names unknown. Lagos. No details available.

12 September 1982 *Nigerian Brewer.* West German registry. 7500 tons. Lagos. Eight pirates boarded at 0350 from modern motor boats and one was seen to fire pistol towards superstructure. Broke open starboard deckhouse door and some empty containers. At 0425 they opened port deckhouse door with bolt-cutter. Left at 0430 but returned at 0435 and fired at chief officer and second officer who were inspecting the main deck. One pirate on deck briefly but left at 0440. Lagos Port Control informed at 0415 on VHF channel 16.

Subsequently one cartridge case found on deck.

October 1982 Name unknown. Port Harcourt. No details available.

October 1982 Name unknown. Freetown. British vessel. No details available.

12 October 1982 *Seki Rokel.* Japanese registry. 12,169-ton Ro-Ro ship. Port Harcourt. Boarded by pirates but no details available.

2 November 1982 *Botany Triumph.* Panama registry. 4594-ton tanker. Lagos. No details available.

11 November 1982 *Midas Apollo.* Liberian registry. 15,493 tons. Off Apapa/Lagos. General cargo ship. Attacked by machine-gun carrying pirates who stole cash and valuables as well as badly beating up most of the officers and crew.

12 November 1982 *Esso Hafnia.* Danish registry. 23,210-ton motor tanker. Dakar. Agent wanted ship to berth as soon as possible as he did not feel the anchorage was safe from thieves. Moved alongside shortly after midnight in petroleum harbour and completed discharge about midnight the following day. Tried to hire local guards but they left shortly after coming on board. Set departure time for 0300. Master went to cabin at 0130 and stretched out on his bunk. At 0200 heard curtain between day and sleeping cabin moving and saw dark figure taking his personal effects out of a drawer. Shouted and started to fight and was stabbed three times in chest, once in face, and once in left arm with some smaller wounds. These injuries were not serious and required total of 12 stitches. Watchman saw negro with knife run down gangway. Ambulance arrived at 0300 and master was taken to hospital and subsequently flown home to Denmark, rejoining ship a month later.

15 November 1982 Name unknown. Apapa/Lagos. No details available.

1 December 1982 *Baltic.* Dutch registry. 2153 tons. Off Apapa/Lagos. Raided by pirates armed with guns at 0515. All the crew locked themselves in the engine room except for the cook who was forced at gun-point to show where the valuables and money were kept. The 2666 ton Dutch reefer vessel *Pacific Marchioness* was nearby and circled the ship, illuminating her with searchlights, and was fired on by the pirates. A patrol boat arrived at 0625 and attacked pirates, one of whom was killed and about four others drowned.

15 December 1982 *Snowfrost*. Greek registry. 2741-ton reefer vessel. Cotonou Roads, 16 miles south of Cotonou harbour in position 6°5.7′N 2°32.7′W. At 0020 two large motor boats with about 15 African pirates approached but were invisible in the moonless night. Six or seven men boarded armed with pistols and knives. Gagged night watchman and beat him as he refused to show the way to the master's cabin. Arrested at least six others including chief officer and posted sentries at accommodation entrances. Three pirates armed with two pistols and a knife forced chief officer to show the way to master's cabin. He saw them and tried to close door and they shot but missed. They beat the master on his face and stomach and took a gold chain and cross from his neck. Opened ship's safe and were surprised to find it empty. Had the free run of the ship and finally departed at about 0300. As the cargo was frozen fish, they found little there but took much else.

27 December 1982 *Vegaland*. Swedish registry. 12,007 ton Ro-Ro ship. Lagos. Anchored Lagos Roads at 0710. Weighed at 1750 to move out to sea to avoid possible pirate attack. At 1953 stopped main engine and lay about 20 miles off shore. Fire pumps kept on to give a water barrier defence. At 2310 men seen climbing up port quarter. Alarm raised and all crew got into their quarters and locked door except for one motor man. However, pirates, firing their weapons, had controlled the bridge. Second mate was shot in leg and eight cartridge cases found subsequently. Port authorities advised on VHF but no assistance as their patrol boat 'out of order'. Finnish ship came close and advised that pirates left the ship at about 0200. Motor man had been threatened with three shots being fired close to his head. He had had to assist pirates in carrying cargo stolen from containers. Finally crew reached the bridge at 0315. Position fixed at 195° 20 nautical miles from East Mole (the entrance piers of Lagos). Pirate boat was 10 metres long, 2 metres wide with 2 outboard engines. At least three pirates had pistols and one a machine pistol. Second mate's wound not dangerous.

27 December 1982 *Transondo Express*. 8710-ton general cargo ship. Anchored 12 nautical miles off Lagos. Firearms used by pirates and crew returned fire. No assistance from shore despite urgent radio appeals.

28 December 1982 *Vegaland*. Swedish registry. 12,007 ton Ro-Ro ship. Twenty miles south of Lagos. Attacked by pirates armed with hand-guns in a fast 10-metre boat with a 'blaze of gunfire'. Second mate slightly wounded. Made off with rolls of cloth.

1983 (exact date unknown). *Seven*. Monrovia.

1983 (exact date unknown) *Export Challenger*. US registry. 12,726-ton general cargo ship. Monrovia. No details available.

4 January 1983 *Athene*. Swedish registry. 260,150-ton tanker. Lagos.

5 January 1983 *Lucie Delmas*. French registry. 24,946 tons. Lagos.

7 January 1983 *Nedlloyd Madras*. Dutch registry. 17,525 tons. Anchored in Lagos Roads. Boarded in daylight and two containers broken into and part contents stolen.

7 January 1983 *Aegis Athenic*. Greek registry. 20,669 tons. Lagos. No details available.

13 January 1983 *Dimitra*. Lagos. No details available.

17 January 1983 *Export Challenger*. US registry. 12,726 tons. Lagos. 12,726-ton general cargo ship. Tinned milk stolen.

17 January 1983 *Anne Sif*. Danish registry. Lagos. At 0515 attacked by 30 pirates in five boats. Broke into deck-stowed cargoes. Patrol boat arrived too late at 0630. 'Bow and arrow' men were on board.

21 January 1983 *Aristée*. French registry. 10,556 tons. Lagos. Attacked at about 2200 by eight pirates armed with revolvers who broke into deck-stowed containers and stole 150 cases of champagne.

25 January 1983 Name unknown. General cargo vessel 4800 tons. Lagos Roads. Armed attack and containers forced open and robbed.

February 1983 *Del Monte*. US registry. 13,428-ton general cargo ship. Takoradi, Ghana. Locals pilfering foodstuffs from ship at anchor.

6 February 1983 *Bruse Jarl.* Norwegian registry. 32,717-ton tanker. Anchored off Lagos. Pirates robbed crew and rifled safe. Two stewardesses reported to be raped.

21 February 1983 Danish ship. 33,401 tons. Lagos.

25 February 1983 *Lonelil.* Benin.

18 March 1983 Danish ship. 33,401 tons. Anchored off Lagos. Attacked by approximately 20 pirates who stole personal effects, stores, provisions, etc, valued at some 200,000 kroner.

19 March 1983 Name unknown. Lagos Roads. Container vessel 7900 tons. Armed attack. First officer punched and wounded. Sailor wounded by bullet in the fibula. Some broken portholes. Port authority asked for help and naval vessel appeared too late.

7 July 1983 Name unknown. Dakar Roads, Senegal. Container vessel 7900 tons. Pirates tried to board ship but were repelled successfully with 'all hands on deck'.

26 July 1983 Name unknown. Lagos. General cargo vessel 3900 grt. Attacked by 15 armed pirates in the morning. Seven containers were forced open and contents stolen from four of them. Lagos port control was informed and armed police appeared, but the pirates escaped.

27-28 July 1983 *La Minera.* Bahamian registry. 6450 tons. Conakry. Aproximately 20 thieves attacked during daylight over two days. The authorities did not intervene. The chief officer and one crew member were attacked on deck. Three large hydraulic jacks were stolen, various stores broken into, and numerous containers broken open and pilfered.

31 August 1983 *Seven.* Italian registry. Monrovia.

31 August 1983 *Lloyd Genova.* Brazilian registry. 14,572 tons. Monrovia.

31 August 1983 *Export Challenger.* US registry. 12,726 tons. Monrovia.

21 September 1983 *Fengtien.* British registry. Lagos.

4 October 1983 *Amazona.* Panamian registry. Benin.

4 October 1983 *Amazona.* Panamian registry. Lagos. 0430. Women pirates raided ships laundry. No details.

13–16 October 1983 Name unknown. Matadi (harbour), Zaire. Container ship 7900 grt. Attacked on each night by gang and containers forced open and robbed. Port authority stated they were unable to provide any help at night.

15 October 1983 Name unknown. Abidjan (inner roads), Ivory Coast. General cargo ship 9500grt. Attacked by about 20 pirates. Watch on duty tied up and robbed. Containers forced open and robbed. SOS sent on VHF and harbour master and port authority informed. No reactions at all.

23 October 1983 Name unknown. Matadi, Zaire. General cargo vessel 15,800 tons. Armed attack and crew member injured. Harbour Master acknowledged a protest but took no action.

25 October 1983 Name unknown. Matadi, Zaire. General cargo vessel 9500 tons. Attacked twice, first at night and then in the morning, by about ten pirates. Eight containers were forced open and robbed and crew members held at gunpoint. Protest lodged with port authority.

4 November 1983 International Federation of Shipmasters' Associations advises that the threat of piracy is still great off the port of Cotonou in Benin. Many ships are sailing or drifting at night without navigation lights and, on passage from Douala to Cotonou, large ships have been encountered sailing without lights, posing a grave threat to safe navigation.

6 November 1983 Name unknown. General cargo vessel 6700 tons. Lagos. Twenty pirates attacked the ship when alongside and loading and made a second attack later on. One crew member injured in the head and shoulders. Harbour police appeared but all the pirates escaped.

---

10 February 1984 *Scilla.* West German registry. 6604-ton general cargo ship. Bonny. Boarded in the Roads about 2100 by 20 pirates armed with knives, boat-hooks, and bottles. Crew repelled them with signal rockets. Another attack made about 20 minutes later by about 15 armed pirates with the same result. Raiders left empty handed though several crew members were hurt by thrown bottles. No assistance given from the shore despite radio calls to Bonny signal station.

19 April 84 *Akindynos C.* Greek registry. 16,499-ton bulk carrier. Freetown. Attacked in the anchorage at 0330 by gang of armed men. Equipment, spares and ropes to value of US $50,000 stolen.

Reports of Piracy in the Singapore Area

During the period from the beginning of 1981 to the end of 1983, a total of 144 incidents were reported to the Singapore authorities. The breakdown given of these is as follows

	1981	1982	1983	**Total**
Inside territorial waters	7	13	8	28
Outside territorial waters	28	32	23	83
Positions unknown	7	9	17	33
Total	**42**	**54**	**48**	**144**

Reports listed below include all cases which have come to light to the Singapore authorities and from other sources of information.

1 August 1980 *Hellespont Pride*. Singapore registry. 89,730 tons. West anchorage off port limits. Probably two intruders came on board at night-time armed with long knives, who threatened the master and third officer and bound their hands before leaving. No resulting injuries. Stole $10,584, two wrist-watches and one gas lighter.

4 March 1981 *Dosina*. Greek registry. 70,361 tons. At anchor.

5 March 1981 *Gerestos*. Greek registry. 62,281 tons. Off Sultan Shoal. No details available.

• Map p80–1

10 April 1981 *Litiopa*. No details available. Event denied by owners.

20 May 1981 *Koei*. Liberian registry. 61,521-ton tanker. Phillip Channel.

26 May 1981 Japanese tanker. Phillip Channel.

16 June 1981 *Vallabhbhai Patel*. Indian registry. 113,925-ton bulk carrier. Phillip Channel. Boarded by pirates who stole cash and valuables.

16 June 1981 *Indian Obo*. Phillip Channel.

17 June 1981 *Vasilikos*. Liberian registry. 141,178-ton tanker. Phillip Channel. Boarded during transit at about 0230 by two pirates who stole some £420 and clothing.

19 June 1981 *Asia Culture.* Liberian registry. 104,942 tons. Phillip Channel.

19 June 1981 *Varenna.* Norwegian registry. 101,600 tons. No details available.

19 June 1981 *Queen Sapphire.* Panamanian registry. 27,852 tons. Phillip Channel.

16 July 1981 *Kenyo Maru.* Japanese registry. Phillip Channel.

17 July 1981 *Contender Argent.* British registry. 22,000-ton Ro-Ro vessel. Twenty miles south-west of Singapore. Boarded by local pirates who stole money, believed to be $30,000.

25 July 1981 *Nedlloyd Main.* Dutch registry. 11,735 tons. Phillip Channel.

27 July 1981 *British Beech.* British registry. 21,093-ton tanker. Phillip Channel. Boarded by local pirates who stole money.

13 August 1981 *Kasuga Maru.* Japanese registry. Phillip Channel.

14 August 1981 *Sea Lion.* Japanese registry. 3128 tons. Phillip Channel.

17 August 1981 *Nedlloyd Weser.* Dutch registry. 7989 tons. Phillip Channel.

17 August 1981 *Sinope.* Indonesian registry. 1650-ton cargo ship. Phillip Channel. Money stolen.

17 August 1981 *Inabukwa.* Indonesian registry. 980-ton general cargo ship. Phillip Channel. Money stolen.

19 August 1981 *Pioneer.* Phillip Channel.

23 August 1981 *Corsicana.* British registry. 29,960 tons. About 2235 hours. In Phillip Channel eastbound at 15 knots adjacent to Pu Takong Kechil island. Three men boarded armed with knives and axes and ran up the bridge ladder. One seized the master (who had no warning at all) who was forced to open the safe in his cabin and some £4000 was stolen. The remaining two pirates remained on the bridge where one stood over the helmsman. The second officer had to fix his position and did so despite warning by the pirates not to. The attackers cut the bridge telephone lines. The deck lights were switched on a few minutes after they left but no sign remained.

September 1981 *Mount Newman.* British registry. 119,500 tons. West Jurong anchorage.

2 September 1981 *Mammoth Monarch.* Liberian registry. 90,900-tons tanker. Phillip Channel eastbound at 12 knots. Raided at 0130. Number of pirates unknown. No crew injury. Stole ship's safe and $7,909 and drugs.

17 September 1981 *Fort Coulonge.* British registry. 30,599 tons. 0425 hours. Western Singapore anchorage at anchor. Three Asian robbers boarded armed with knives similar to Japanese *hara-kiri* swords, and dressed in swimming shorts. Found master asleep in cabin and tied him up and demanded money while they threatened him with their knives. Some belongings and cash stolen but did not get into ship's safe. Left after about ten minutes. Police on board at 0545.

19 September 1981 *Diana.* 81,283-ton tanker. Phillip Channel shortly after leaving Singapore. Attacked by gang of three wearing loincloths, armed with jungle knives, and operating from a speedboat.

20 September 1981 *Hakata Maru.* Probably Japanese registry. 4791-ton general cargo ship. In Phillip Channel shortly after leaving Singapore. Raider seen by crew but he escaped. This was probably the same gang that attacked the *Diana* on the preceding day and they boarded while vessel slowing down to go through channel.

21 September 1981 *Nigeria Venture.* Liberian registry. 18,250 tons. Phillip Channel.

21 September 1981 *Elpida.* Believed to be Greek registry. Phillip Channel.

25 September 1981 *Mount Newman.* British registry. 119,500 tons. West Jurong anchorage.

25 September 1981 *Abbey.* Believed British registry of 118,750 tons. 0335 hours. Singapore anchorage. Boarded by armed pirates and two pairs of binoculars and a chronometer stolen.

29 September 1981 *Kohnan Maru.* Japanese registry. 167,516-ton ore carrier. Singapore harbour. Boarded by five pirates armed with knives who held up the chief officer and ransacked his office and personal belongings and took about $450.

1982 *Agrilia.* Panamanian registry. 13,618 tons. Position not known.

January 1982 Name unknown. Malaysian fishing expedition 30 kilometres off Kota Kinabulu in international waters. Eight pirates armed with guns and machetes circled fishing boat, boarded it, and towed it to a nearby island where it was stripped.

28 January 1982 *Magnificence Venture.* Liberian registry. 26,500 tons. South-west of Singapore.

2 February 1982 *Yuyo Maru.* Japanese registry. 6849 tons. South of Singapore.

5 February 1982 *Chief Dragon.* Taiwanese registry. Position unknown.

27 February 1982 *Crown Atland.* South-west of Singapore.

13 March 1982 *Lei Tsu.* Taiwanese registry. East of Singapore.

16 March 1982 *Asian Hawk.* Panamanian registry. 20,260 tons. South-west of Singapore.

18 March 1982 *Neptune Turquoise.* Singapore registry. 15,069 tons. 0330 hours. Position 1.2°N 105°9'E passing through Singapore Straits at 8 knots. Master's wife held at knife-point in cabin while three men, probably Indonesians, tried to break safe open. Failed and only stole a stereo system. Left without being discovered.

19 March 1982 *Miwon Line.* South Korean registry. 6096 tons. Position unknown.

21 March 1982 *Frankfurt Express.* Panamanian registry. 16,547 tons. South of Singapore.

21 March 1982 *Piolet Island.* South-west of Singapore.

23 March 1982 *Norman.* Position unknown.

12 April 1982 *Danimar.* Panamanian registry. 20,565-ton tanker. Five pirates boarded. No details available.

27 April 1982 *Montauk Gannet.* Phillip Channel.

25 May 1982 *Divine Valley.* Panamanian registry. 60,960-ton tanker. West Jurong anchorage. Five pirates stole $8,325 in cash, and valuables.

27 May 1982 *Rose Garden Maru*. Japanese registry. 4229-ton tanker. Off Buffalo Rock eastbound. Four pirates stole $1,317.

6 June 1982 *Fellow Wealth*. Panamian registry. 6147-ton cargo ship. South-west of Singapore. Three pirates stole $200-worth of cargo.

17 June 1982 *Biscay*. Phillip Channel.

21 July 1982 *World Cliff*. Liberian registry. 88,272-ton tanker. Early morning hours. Approaching Sultan Shoal to pick up pilot *en route* for Singapore. Boarded by four men armed with knives over the stern, despite this being flood lit. Surprised chief officer in his cabin and tied him up and stole his personal belongings. Also raided master's cabin and removed safe and stole other items.

6 August 1982 *Beauxarts*. Panamanian registry. 3410-ton tanker. Phillip Channel westbound. Four pirates stole £1,500.

8 August 1982 *Al Wattyah*. Kuwaiti registry. 24,032-ton container ship. South-west of Singapore, westbound. Two or three pirates stole cash and personal effects.

11 August 1982 *Agrilia*. Panamanian registry. 13,616-ton general cargo ship. Phillip Channel. Eight pirates stole an $89 watch.

12 August 1982 *Tulip*. Panamanian registry. 16,382-ton general cargo ship. Around daybreak, passing Sultan Shoal. Four men, armed with guns, were sighted on board and alarm raised. They were frightened off without anything being taken.

12 August 1982 *Port Latta Maru*. Japanese registry. 93,355 tons. Phillip Channel.

12 August 1982 *Nippo Maru*. Japanese registry. Bulk carrier. Phillip Channel. $650 stolen.

19 August 1982 *Homeria*. Five miles east of Singapore. 30,000-ton cargo ship. $15,650 stolen.

25 August 1982 *Lanka Siri*. Sri Lankan registry. 3831-ton container ship. About 0515 hours, approaching Singapore, some 15–20 miles off in Phillip Channel adjacent to Eastern Pilot Boarding Grounds near St John's light. Seven pirates boarded without being seen. Master's wife and child asleep in his cabin and pirates entered his day room without noticing them. Master returned to his cabin and heard noise and saw through the door pirates armed with swords, knives, and other weapons. Returned to bridge and sounded alarm. Pirates ran for safety.

25 August 1982 *Seiwa Maru.* Phillip Channel. Cargo ship. Attack repelled.

26 August 1982 *Asian Rose.* Japanese registry. 6203 tons. Batu Berhanti eastbound. One pirate stole $1,962.

29 August 1982 *Bunga Dahlia.* Malaysian registry. 5362-ton container ship. 0615 hours. Phillip Channel almost abeam of Buffalo Rock. Small boat 8 metres long with outboard engine running parallel about 5 metres away. Boat was illuminated and hailed but two intruders were already on board. Bridge entrances locked and alarm sounded. Shortly thereafter the last pirate seen jumping down into the boat. Ship's safe and some personal belongings stolen from master's cabin.

2 September 1982 *Kasuga Maru.* Japanese registry. Phillip Channel. Cargo vessel. Abortive pirate raid.

9 September 1982 *Benvalla.* British registry. 8319-ton container ship. Off Singapore. Sailed from Singapore at 0155 and passed through eastern Singapore Strait. At 0620 the master found his cabin had been ransacked and safe emptied of all valuables. A four fathom length of rope had been cut and hung over the stern where presumably the thieves made their escape. Total loss of $10,975.

15 September 1982 *Palmstar Orchid.* Singapore registry. 96,530-ton tanker. Phillip Channel. Raided at 0215–0345. Number of pirates unknown. No crew injury. Stole ship's safe and $4,435 and medicines.

15 September 1982 *Japan Stork.* Japanese registry. 80,750-ton tanker. Phillip Channel.

15 September 1982 *Iso Kasuma.* Phillip Channel. Tanker. Five pirates stole $3,240.

16 September 1982 *Grand Globe.* Liberian registry. 19,184-ton bulk carrier. South-east of Singapore, eastbound. Four pirates stole $300.

16 September 1982 *Meiji Maru.* Japanese registry. 15,447-ton bulk carrier. Phillip Channel. Pirates driven off.

17 September 1982 *San Bruno.* Philippine registry. 8,575-ton reefer. Five pirates boarded.

19 September 1982 *World Radiance.* Liberian registry. 141,671 ton tanker. South-east of Singapore, eastbound. Money stolen.

20 September 1982 *Neptune Leo.* Singapore registry. 96,531-ton tanker. Position 01°13.3'N 103°55.5'E. Raided just after midnight. Number of intruders not known. No crew injury or drugs stolen although one crew member chased with a machete. Stole complete ship's safe and $17,292.

23 September 1982 *Am Carrier.* Japanese registry. 6135-ton bulk carrier. Position unknown. Medical equipment stolen.

29 September 1982 *Golar Kanto.* Liberian registry. 219,175-ton tanker. East of Singapore. Proceeding at slow speed and taking stores from a supply launch. At least three men boarded undetected and stole master's safe containing $30,000.

16 October 1982 *Yick Wing.* Bulk carrier. South-west of Singapore. Boarded by pirates.

17 October 1982 *Hua Hin.* Tanker. Position unknown. Television and watch stolen.

22 October 1982 *Thai Yung.* Taiwanese registry. 7845-ton general cargo ship. Phillip Channel. Captain injured and one watch stolen.

22 October 1982 *Plata.* West German registry. 13,005-ton container ship. Phillip Channel.

22 October 1982 *Bonvoy.* Honduran registry. 3499-ton tanker. South-east Singapore. Four pirates robbed the crew.

24 October 1982 *Sincere.* Off Singapore. No details available.

26 October 1982 *Ratana Bhum.* Probably Indian registry. 3210-ton general cargo ship. Off Singapore. Radio and $90 stolen.

27 October 1982 *Eiwa Maru.* Japanese registry. 3277-ton tanker. Phillip Channel. Attacked by four pirates armed with knives who held up the crew, ransacked the vessel and stole cash.

29 October 1982 *Hand Ming.* Panamanian registry. 9135 ton bulk carrier. Singapore area eastbound. Four pirates stole $50,000.

1 November 1982 *Kota Suria*. Container ship. Off Singapore. Four pirates stole $3,500.

9 November 1982 *St Paulia*. Panamanian registry. 28,587-ton tanker. Singapore area eastbound. Four pirates stole $1,550.

10 November 1982 *Cys Knight*. Liberian registry. 36,829-ton tanker. East of Singapore eastbound. Three pirates boarded.

10 November 1982 *Seizan Maru*. Liberian registry. 45,886-ton general cargo ship. South-west of Singapore eastbound. Cash stolen.

11 November 1982 *Sivand*. Iranian registry. 218,587-ton tanker. South-west of Singapore eastbound. No details available.

12 November 1982 *Stolt Condor*. Liberian registry. 36,613-ton tanker. Eastbound, position unknown. Valuables and $13,000 stolen.

12 November 1982 *Mobil Endurance*. 33,225-ton tanker. Position not known, westbound. Valuables and $100 stolen.

12 November 1982 *Shenandoah*. Greek registry. 27,028-ton bulk carrier. South-west of Singapore eastbound. Six pirates stole $5,500.

12 November 1982 *Great Fortune*. South-east of Singapore eastbound. Bulk carrier. No details available.

15 November 1982 *Yuyo Maru*. Japanese registry. Tanker. Singapore area eastbound. No details available.

26 November 1982 *Tomoe*. Phillip Channel. Tanker. Safe stolen.

29 November 1982 *Eastern Virgo*. Phillip Channel. 6229-ton general cargo ship. $4,500 cash stolen.

January 1983 *Spartan*. US registry. Off Singapore, position unknown. Attacked but pirates repulsed.

10 January 1983 *Diamond Glory*. Panamanian registry. 51,538 tons. 01°16′N 104°12′E. 0115 hours. Some cash and a video camera were stolen, value unknown.

10 January 1983 *Sealift Arctic*. US registry. 27,648 tons. 0020 hours. 01°14.5′N 104°03′E. Seven male intruders, one of whom was armed, boarded the vessel. Master's cabin looted. 13in close circuit television, credit card and American Express card stolen. Value unknown.

13 January 1983 *Bokuho.* Panamanian registry. 60,961 tons. 0215. Buffalo Rocks in Indonesian waters. Two pirates boarded and $3,000 stolen.

16 January 1983 *South Sea.* Singapore registry. 2400 tons. 0215. Eight miles east of Peak Island in Indonesian waters. Four Indonesians boarded and stole HK $700 and US $1,600.

23 January 1983 *Magnificence Venture.* Liberian registry. 26,500 tons. 0400 hours. One nautical mile off Batu Berhenti in Indonesian waters. Six armed intruders. Goods, $500, two rings, a watch, and a radio stolen, value unknown.

2 February 1983 *Yuyo Maru.* Japanese registry. 6849-ton tanker. 0540 hours. 1°,11.7'N 103°,52.5'E in Indonesian waters. Six pirates boarded and stole 118,165 Japanese Yen and about $1,027.

5 February 1983 *Chief Dragon.* Taiwanese registry. 6849 tons. 0250 hours. Passing through Straits of Singapore, exact position not known. 285,000 Japanese Yen, $2,850, strong-box and one set of cassettes stolen, value unknown.

7 February 1983 *Sea Silk Road.* Japanese registry. 59,999 tons. South-east of Singapore.

7 February 1983 *Crown Atland.* Swedish registry. Eastern Petroleum Anchorage eastbound. 0420 hours. Four pirates boarded and some cash and other items stolen.

13 March 1983 *Lei Tsu.* Taiwanese registry. 98,969 tons. 0300 hours. Ten miles east of Horsbrugh lighthouse. Two pirates boarded armed with long knives and stole $350.

13 March 1983 *Archilles.* Position unknown.

15 March 1983 *Orco Trader.* Liberian registry. 129,882 tons. 3215 hours. Eastbound channel of the separation scheme. Captain went to his cabin from bridge and met six pirates all carrying large knives. He was seized but managed to escape although bleeding from cut on the nose. Alarm sounded and pirates escaped. One wrist-watch stolen.

16 March 1983 *Asian Hawk.* Panamanian registry. 20,260 tons.

Between 0100 and 0500 hours. Between Horsburgh lighthouse and Phillip Channel. $4,182 stolen.

18 March 1983 *Neptune Turquoise.* Singapore registry. 15,069 tons. 0400 hours. 20 nautical miles east of Singapore. One Hi-Fi system stolen.

18 March 1983 *Aura Bravery.* Liberian registry. 0230 hours. At sea off Raffles lighthouse; exact location not known. One cassette radio player and camera stolen.

19 March 1983 *Miwon.* South Korean registry. 6096 tons. 2300 hours. Two nautical miles south-west of Peak Island. Radio, $110, Casio calculator, and some clothing stolen.

21 March 1983 *Piolet Island.* 0540 hours. Two miles off Palau Satuma and Raffles lighthouse, westbound. Some cash and a long sword stolen.

21 March 1983 *Frankfurt Express.* Panamanian registry. 16,547 tons. 0110 hours. At sea off Buffalo Rocks. Some property stolen.

23 March 1983 *Stolt Crown.* Liberian registry. 18,130 tons. Westbound, position unknown.

25 March 1983 *Narnian Sea.* British registry. 81,250 tons. 1.2 miles north-north-east of Brothers light. 0330. Ship was making 14 knots *en route* to Manila Bay. Poop deck was fully floodlit with two crew members on patrol. Suddenly one reported three intruders on the poop deck. They had long knives, black pouches strapped around their torsos, black bandages over their foreheads, and were barefoot. They had come on board by grappling hook over the stern (the ship had 7.3 metres freeboard) and had unwound 30 feet of 8-inch mooring rope from the drum stowage, cut if off, and were passing it back over the stern to assist others to get on board. A crew member was threatened with a knife as pirates climbed back down over the stern and made off in a speedboat. This was 20–25 feet long with a well silenced and powerful engine. It contained seven men.

23 March 1983 *Norman.* Panamanian registry. Two miles off Pulau Kukub in Malaysian waters. $1,600 stolen.

March 1983 *M T Narian.* 4.5 miles from Brothers Lighthouse in Straits of Malacca. Nothing stolen.

24 March 1983 *African Express.* Dutch registry. 15,210 tons. 0815 hours. Straits of Malacca. £75,841 worth of Chinese dollars, US $200, 175 Dutch guilders, Omega watch, and cassette recorder stolen.

5 April 1983 *Pegasus Pride.* South Korean registry. 5615 tons. 2308 hours. Eastbound separation lane. Rolex watch, cassette player, handbag, fountain pen, wallet, two cigarette lighters, and $2,580 stolen from safe.

7 April 1983 *Pacific Export.* 0315 hours. Phillip Channel. Some personal belongings stolen and $3,000.

7 April 1983 *Strathconon.* Singapore registry. 0430 hours. Westbound traffic separation scheme two miles from Raffles lighthouse. £366, radio, and some personal belongings stolen.

7 April 1983 *Setco Mammoth.* 2220 hours. Travellers cheques worth $11,000. $300, radio, television, video recorder, two wrist-watches, gold coloured chain, and wedding ring stolen.

13 April 1983 *Sun Grace.* 2327 hours. 3.25 miles off Pulau Kukup. Items stolen not known.

13 April 1983 *Toyo Fujimaru.* Japanese registry. Phillip Channel in position 1°12.3'N 103°54.5'E. Pirates sighted the ship's crew and escaped without stealing anything.

14 April 1983 *Bunga Mas.* Malaysian registry. 4392 tons. 0250 hours. At sea off Phillip Channel. Two pirates boarded and stole some $3876.

14 April 1983 *Skoun Ambassador.* 2320 hours. Malacca Straits. 50,000 Japanese Yen, US $700, $100, Malaysian $50, camera, cassette player, and some personal belongings stolen.

18 April 1983 *Van er Stel.* 0400–0600 hours. Main Straits of Singapore, exact location unknown. HK $400, 15,000 Japanese Yen, jade bracelet, coral brooch, communication receiver, and four micro Hi-Fi sets stolen.

22 April 1983 *Yumiko.* Panamanian registry. 5950 tons. 0155 hours. 080 degrees, 6.5 miles from St John Island eastbound in Indonesian waters. $2665 and wrist-watch stolen.

4 May 1983 *Montauk Gannet.* Phillip Channel. Master surprised in cabin by two men who put knife to his throat. Took ship's safe and some other belongings and lowered them to their speedboat over the stern. Safe contained $1650 and 300 Japanese Yen.

4 May 1983 *Palmstar Cherry*. Singapore registry. 96,530 tons. 0504 hours. 01°,04′N 103°,40′E eight miles south-west of Raffles lighthouse. Nine armed pirates boarded and $300–$400 stolen from master's cabin.

8 May 1983 *Aurora Glory* 0300–0430 hours. 1.5 miles south of Port Takong lighthouse, Phillip Channel. Safe box containing $1500 stolen.

12 May 1983 *Southern Cruiser*. 2200–2300 hours. 01°02′N 103°39′E Phillip Channel. Cash, cassette recorder, camera, and watch stolen from master's cabin.

13 May 1983 *Esther Lu*. Panamanian registry. 8395 tons. 0300 hours. Three miles east of Raffles lighthouse (outside port limits). Empty safe reported missing from master's cabin.

18 May 1983 *Benvalla*. British registry. 8319 tons. 031° 5 miles from Brothers Light at 13.5 knots. A native sampan was sighted and illuminated but intruders already on board. Alarm sounded and four intruders ran aft and climbed down lengths which had been cut off mooring lines and hung over the stern. Another four intruders may have been seen to make total of eight. Wrist-watch stolen from chief engineer's cabin.

19 May 1983 *An Ping*. West of Singapore. No details.

2 June 1983 *Benvalla*. British registry. 8319 tons. Brothers Light. No details available.

24 June 1983 *Lanka Siri*. Sri Lankan registry. South-west of Singapore.

1 July 1983 *Chie Maru*. Japanese registry. 7621 tons. Straits of Malacca. Attacked by five pirates armed with machetes shortly after midnight. Stole some £1800 and personal goods from master and crew

7 July 1983 *Stena Oceanica*. Swedish registry. 41,256 tons. 2320 hours. Phillip Channel in position 030° 1 mile from Pu Takong Kechil light at 13 knots. At 2330 chief officer reported master's office ransacked and found that ship's safe had been removed as well as some personal goods. Radio officer found on poop deck with hands tied and had been held at knife-point by three men during the raid. Reported that he had surprised five men. Pirates believed to have boarded at about 2255 when ship was making 13 knots. They were on board for about 30 minutes in all.

8 July 1983 *Mega Taurus*. Japanese registry. 30,413 tons. Straits of Malacca. Attacked in the early hours by five pirates armed with machetes who robbed Master of 80,000 Yen, Canadian $20 and a radio.

21 July 1983 Name Unknown. Last reported incident for 1983.

5 August 1983 Indonesian oil tanker. Phillip Channel 10 miles south of Singapore. Armed pirates broke into safe and stole about $15,000 cash. Five members of the gang were later arrested by Indonesian police at their base at Batam Island in the Riau Archipelago. The police seized weapons, jewellery, and other valuables.

---

19 March 1984 Name Unknown. Five miles from Brothers Light. 0300. Five men boarded using mooring ropes. General alarm sounded and pirate's boat illuminated by Aldis lamp. Departed with chief engineer's wrist-watch and a few fathoms of mooring rope.

3 June 1984 Name unknown. 0450 hours. Just west of Buffalo Rock in westbound channel. Believed to be the first incident recorded in 1984.

25 June 1984 Unknown vessel. No details other than in Singapore area at sea.

29 June 1984 Unknown vessel. 0100 hours. Eastbound lane south-east of Bukit Pengerang.

25 July 1984 Name unknown. 0255 hours. Just north-west of Buffalo Rocks.

3 August 1984 Name unknown. 0005 hours. Westbound lane south-south-east of Changi airport.

4 August 1984 Name unknown. 0300 hours. Westbound lane south of Bukit Pengerang and south-east of Changi airport.

6 August 1984 Name unknown. 0025 hours. Eastbound channel South-South-East of Bukit Pengerang.

22 August 1984 Note from a member of the Port of Singapore Authority that 'the number of piracy incidents has increased dramatically in the last few months. The pirates appear to have resumed their operations after a prolonged period of inactivity.'

Reports of Piracy in the Gulf of Siam and Thailand Area

The following information concerning the attempts of Vietnamese refugees endeavouring to escape to Thailand has been extracted mainly from the *Bangkok Post* with additional information from the United Nations High Commission for Refugees (UNHCR) and other sources.

1979

May	Over 2000 refugees arriving in Thailand each month.
July	Hanoi agrees to limit the numbers of refugees which fell to 200 a month temporarily.
November 1979	910 refugees landed with the good weather.

1980

January 1–10	499 refugees landed in Thailand in 10 days.
1980	77% of boats landing were attacked. Some reports of 6000 refugees landing each month with 2000 in Malaysia alone in April.
1981	15,598 Vietnamese emigrated. 77% of boats attacked. Of these, about 13,000 came to southern Thailand and over 80% of their boats were attacked on average 3.5 times each.
1982	5913 refugees emigrated. 65% of boats attacked.
1983	3383 refugees emigrated. 56% of boats attacked.

January to June 1984 47% of boats attacked.
1. Between May 1982 and April 1983, 463 boats landed in Thailand and Malaysia. 196 had been attacked; 56 people died;

228 women were raped; and 133 women were abducted.

2. Private organisations have funded boats to assist the refugees:

1978	USA	*Akuna I*
1978–81	USA	*Seasweep*
1979–80	France	*Ile de Lumiere*
1980–82	France	*Goele*
1979–80	Norway	*Lysekild*
1980–82	Germany	*Cap Anamur*
1980–81	Germany	*Flora*
1981–84	USA	*Akuna I Akuna II Akuna III*
1981–83	Swiss	*Akuna II Akuna III Herta S*

Incidents noted:

November 1979 Nine bodies found washed ashore near Nakorn Si Thammaret about 50 kilometres from Kra island where Thai fishermen had reported people being raped and murdered earlier in the month. Believed to be murdered refugees but could have been from Thai fishing boat which had capsized in storm. Numerous complaints also received of Thai fishermen being robbed of their catch and valuables with some incidents occurring less than 3000 metres off coast in officially restricted waters.

• Map p82–3

November 1979 Seven Thais arrested for raping Vietnamese women on Kra island.

November 1979 16 refugees killed by pirates.

3 December 1979 Boat with 100 people rammed by 2 pirate boats and 80 drowned. 20 survivors taken to Kra where women were raped repeatedly during several days of captivity.

31 December 1979 Island of Koh Kra off southern Thailand. Three refugee boats with 191 refugees seen by four pirate boats. 50 pirates boarded and beat up men using clubs. Survivors taken to Kra island and turned loose. Word spread through pirate community and dozens of other pirates turned up to rape and hunt at will. One eight-year-old girl reported she was raped by 100 men during the week she and 120 other survivors were held on Kra. This brought to 166 the numbers of boat people killed since mid-November.

1 February 1980 Island of Koh Kra. In the past 12 weeks, 200 refugees seeking haven were butchered and some clubbed to death. Hundreds of girls raped by pirates who stalk them through the island's lush undergrowth. One 10-year-old raped eight times and seen by eye-witnesses. One had three gold teeth and the pirates tried to remove them by smashing with a rifle butt and then with pliers, and then raped his 15-year-old daughter. UNHCR received document from Vietnamese couple detailing 20 terror-filled days with no food except that brought daily by the pirates. At one point they counted 47 pirate boats anchored in Kra's inlet.

February 1980 50 people, all related, left Vietnam in small fishing boat. After three days at sea they met a freighter whose crew robbed them. A few days later a second gang of pirates took what was left of their valuables. A third gang smashed their engine and threw the freshwater overboard. Girls aged from 15 to 18 were herded on to pirate boat and repeatedly raped until interrupted by a passing boat. All girls returned to refugee boat except three who have not been heard of since. Reward of 150,000 baht being offered by relate Hong Kong ship owner.

March 1980 300 kilometres north-east of Kuala Lumpur and close to refugee camp at Pulau Bidong where some 12,000 refugees are currently housed. The refugees were stopped on Monday afternoon by a boat with nine pirates on board – seven men, a woman, and a teenager. Three of these boarded the refugee boat armed with a hook, a rake, and a knife. They were pushed overboard and Molotov cocktails thrown at the pirate boat which pulled away. It continued the pursuit and a second pirate boat was seen in the evening with about eight people on board. Later on Monday one of these pirate boats rammed the refugee boat causing it to break up. Refugees tried to get on board the pirate boat but they allowed only the women and a few children in, leaving the others to drown. Two survivors swam ashore and 14 were rescued by Malaysian fishing boats.

22 March 1980 Two pirate boats attacked small wooden boat with 73 refugees. There were only 16 survivors.

April 1980 Kuala Lumpur. Reported that Malaysian Navy captured pirate boat which had robbed Vietnamese refugee boat. This is the first to be captured and believed to be a Thai fishing boat. Second Thai boat also caught and believed to be involved in piracy. Identified by refugees brought from camp at Pulau Bidong 32 kilometres north of Kuala Trengganu. During last three months, about 20% of all refugee boats coming across South China Sea had been attacked with some involving brutal rape, murder and robbery within Malaysian territorial waters. Some 80 Vietnamese refugee boats reached Malaysian shores this year with about 2500 people on board.

29 June 1980 Seven Thai fishermen sentenced to 8 to 24 years imprisonment for raping Vietnamese refugees on Kra island. These were the first sentences known to have been passed against pirates by a Thai court.

September 1980 UNHCR report. Some refugees stop voluntarily in Koh Kra but the majority have been brought there by pirates who return day after day to hunt and rape them. Koh Kra island is five square kilometres of rock and jungle, with two beaches of white coral. One women was severely burned when pirates set fire to hillside to flush her out of hiding. Another cowered for days in a cave until crabs had torn much of the flesh off her legs. A young girl died after gang-rape. Over 160 persons died on Koh Kra in the summer of 1979. The UNHCR hired fishing boats and rescued some 1,250 persons in the same period and there are press reports that the Thai police co-operated with them. The UNHCR now has its own unarmed ocean-going speed boat to visit the island and alert the authorities by radio. Nevertheless those leaving the island planted notices such as 'First you will be given something to eat; then everything will be taken away from you, even your clothes. They will rape you, boatload after boatload; they will come in their hundreds and rape you in turn. Then they will kill you.'

1981 A fishing trawler near Kra island was attacked by six pirates who demanded that the catch be transferred to their boat and then forced the crew to lie down on their stomachs when they shot each in the head. One man escaped by feigning death.

1981 Six pirates in a trawler rammed a boat in the Gulf of Thailand but it was a naval anti-piracy boat which they had thought to be a fishing boat. All were arrested and came from Nakhon Si Thammarat Province.

January 1981 15 naked bodies found washed up in Songkhla Province beach. Believed to be fishermen who could have been attacked by pirates, or smugglers who got involved in a dispute with another smuggling gang. One body headless, another with fractured skull, and all badly bruised.

January 1981 8 boat people landed in Songkhla. Had left Vietnam on 1 January as part of group of 44, but the other 36 were killed during a pirate attack. Eight had survived by pretending to be dead and all were wounded. They had been attacked on third day out from Kiang Yang and their valuables stolen. Later the same day they were attacked by group who started firing at them.

April 1981 A trawler came to Chaimongkol fishing pier in Muang District to sell a full catch but was not one of pier owner's usual customers nor registered in Surat Thani Province. When he would not buy their fish, they asked for an advance so as to be able to repair their engine. Blood stains were seen on board so the police were informed. All nine crew jumped into water but seven were arrested. Understood that four alleged pirates encouraged five crew members to rob the trawler near Koh Samui as it was returning to Samut Sakhon with a full catch. The skipper, mechanic and cook were killed and thrown overboard.

June 1981 Vietnamese pirates in five craft attacked two Thai fishing boats about 20 kilometres off Pattani coast. Pirates were in green uniforms, spoke Vietnamese, and were armed with M16 rifles. They started shooting at Thai boats, overpowered the crews, and took away their catch of about 4000 kilogrammes.

August 1981 Malaysians have detained 54 boats in past month in joint campaign with Thai Marine police. Also said that a Thai syndicate, possibly with co-operation from Malaysians, is robbing Malaysian fishermen of their boats and detaining them for ransom. This syndicate usually collected protection money from fishermen and their boats were taken away if they failed to pay. The boundary between Malaysian and Thai waters is not well known and fishermen become an easy prey for pirates if they enter Thai waters.

September 1981 Four Thai fishermen were killed and four seriously wounded when two fishing trawlers attacked in the Gulf of Thailand about ten miles off Laem Singh by a third trawler which had been captured earlier by Vietnamese troops. These men opened fire with sub-machine guns and seized the two Thai trawlers but handed over the survivors and dead to another Thai trawler.

October 1981 *Cap Anamur*. 5300-ton freighter which had so far rescued 7900 boat people from piracy and drowning reported rescue of 98 people from one craft who were taken to Palawan in the Philippines.

October 1981 Fishing trawler skipper arrested while raping 15-year-old Vietnamese girl. Discovered by navy boat on routine patrol who investigated trawler anchored along Songkhla coastline and heard scream from lower cabin. Girl said she and 41 others had escaped in October 1980 and been attacked three times. When there were no valuables left, pirates took turns to rape five girls on board and took them away with them. Girls were passed from one fishing trawler to another and she herself had been given to two fishing trawler crewmen and been raped six times by them before the Navy boat rescued her.

October 1981 Eight persons arrested in Pattani. Suspects taken after trawler *Po Darunee* reported being seized by eight armed men while fishing. They reportedly confessed to robbing several boats along the coast but also suspected of preying on refugees drifting on high seas.

December 1981 All nine crewmen killed in fishing boat returning from Burma by seven men armed with M 16 rifles in long tall boat. After stripping the nine crewmen of their belongings worth about 100,000 baht, they were shot and thrown overboard. A 33-year-old woman was put ashore at Tarukrut island, eight kilometres away. One suspect detained for questioning.

24 December 1981 48 boat people landed on the shore of Songkhla Lake after four days on high seas when they had been attacked three times by pirates.

January 1982 Boat attacked four times. During the last attack, pirates armed with knives and grappling hooks threw woman's husband and 23 other men overboard to drown. Her three children, including three-month-old baby, were also drowned. She was then raped for 11 days.

January 1982 Seventeen-year-old raped repeatedly by seven men before being set adrift in a bamboo basket. Picked up again two days later and raped again and set afloat before being rescued by friendly fishermen.

January 1982 Five Thai pirates arrested by Malaysian police. Two Malaysian trawlers fishing north of Penang off Langkawi Island 500 kilometres north-west of Kuala Lumpur when five Thai pirates came alongside in a sampan. They took the trawlers and ordered the fishermen into their sampan. When the fishermen reached the shore they informed the police who found the trawlers 16 kilometres south of Langkawi island and opened fire until they surrendered. Later reports are that 13 suspected pirates were arrested near Langkawi island.

January 1982 West German refugee ship *Cap Anamur* freed 99 Vietnamese boat people from pirates. The refugee vessel had originally carried 124 persons when the pirates attacked.

February 1982 Two Thai trawlers and their crews were seized by pirates believed to be Vietnamese when fishing off Muang district. One crew was 25 men strong. Gang of 20 men seized both boats and escaped towards Vietnamese waters some 430 kilometres to the north-east.

March 1982 German refugee ship *Cap Anamur* picked up eight women refugees thrown overboard by a pirate boat it had trailed. Another 11 women seen on pirate boat but could not be rescued. *Cap Anamur* had rescued over 9000 Vietnamese and was the only private organisation operating a rescue service in this area in 1982.

April 1982 Five Thai trawlers fishing 34 nautical miles off island of Obi when Vietnamese patrol boats opened fire with 40mm, 20mm, and AK47 rifles. One was sunk, one captured, and three escaped.

2 April 1982 Nine-man gang attacked small fishing boat near island of An Thong. Two crewmen shot dead and another seriously wounded. The following day the same gang robbed a fishing boat and a trawler and killed three crew. Gang had also robbed Vietnamese boat people. Two men arrested and the remainder being sought.

July 1983 Vietnamese boat left Vung Tau on 29 July with 28 people. 7 or 8 pirates rammed it shortly after with a radar equipped fishing boat and threw most of Vietnamese into sea where they were left to drown. Gold and valuables stolen. Women raped repeatedly. Only two known survivors.

November 1983 Pulau Redang off north-eastern state of Trengganu. Two Vietnamese women, aged 17 and 31, jumped off trawler and swam to Pulau Redang. More than 100 Thai fishermen in 18 trawlers approached the island to demand the return of the women. When a Malaysian naval boat approached, the blockade of trawlers stopped it from approaching and it had to fire several warning shots.

January 1984 16 people in a small boat were attacked on second day out in Gulf of Thailand. All robbed and women taken on board pirate vessel and repeatedly raped for 17 hours.

21 January 1984 More than 10 fishing boats robbed in Surat Thani, Chumphon and Nakhon Si Thammarat provinces since the beginning of January and one crewman murdered.

23 January 1984 Two suspected pirates arrested in Punpin District. Only two cases of piracy in the province since the previous October when a notorious gang of seven had been arrested.

24 January 1984 Surat Thani. About 15 trawlers robbed, and one crew member murdered, since the start of the year in the provinces of Surat Thani. Chumphon and Nakhon Si Thammarat. Four combined police task-forces have been set up in this district to combat piracy.

1 February 1984 UNHCR Representative in Kuala Lumpur reported pirates have killed at least 104 Vietnamese refugees in past three months. Seven refugees are still missing and 22 have been abducted. Figures do not include victims on boats which have been sunk. Most pirates are Thais operating in international waters. They are often on high-powered boats and moor alongside refugee boats for armed robbery.

17 February 1984 Thai navy stepped up anti-piracy patrols about three months previously but no arrests made. Navy patrols guarding areas 12 miles off shore had not encountered any.

16 February 1984 Bangkok Shipowners and Agents Association. In past two months five merchant ships (leaving

Bangkok) had been raided by speedboat pirates – three ships were bound for Japan and two for Singapore. These boats resembled police patrol boats and are about 20 metres long and manned by 15–20 armed men. They have an average speed of 30–40 knots and are faster than the police boats. Usually they board ships at night and head straight for the containers holding the cargo they want and know exactly which container to go to. They then throw the goods overboard to their boat. Pirates attacked 15 kilometres beyond Pak Nam pilot station; near Samet Island off Rayong, near Juang Island off Si Racha and off Sattahip in Chon Buri Province. Inbound cargo has also been taken.

Early 1984 Thai Government sources reported a new development. A gang of pirates using specially designed speedboats were attacking passenger and merchant vessels in the Gulf of Thailand. The pirates usually operate in groups of 15 to 20 and have made a number of recent attacks. Marine police were having particular difficulty in countering these as the pirate craft are faster than police and navy craft.

1985 Lloyd's Nautical Year Book. Pirates around coasts of Thailand have killed 1376, raped 2283, and abducted 592.

Reports of Piracy in the Philippines Area

The pirates in the Indonesian and Philippine archipelago are full time predators. They are the heirs of the gentlemen described 1500 years ago by Fa Hsien in warning his compatriots of 'many pirates who, coming on you suddenly, destroy everything'. Full reports are difficult to come by and the incidents listed below clearly form only a minor proportion of those which have actually occurred.

• Map p82–3

14 May 1980 *Oriental Ambassador*. British registry. 24,037 tons. Manila Bay off Limay Point. Boarded by gang called 'Morning Glory' while sheltering in the bay. The gang were armed with automatic weapons and the master was held up in his cabin while they demanded the key to the safe. He was shot with a burst from an Armalite rifle while probably trying to push a revolver away from his neck. A Hong Kong engineer was also wounded. The gang escaped empty handed and five of the eight were later caught.

25 June 1980 *Siako.* Manila Bay. Local pirates stole cash and valuables.

---

6 July 1981 *Iliana Bay.* Near Bocana, Cotabato City, Philippines. Hijacked by either local terrorists or pirates who forced ship to proceed to another destination to unload its cargo of rice. Master reportedly stabbed to death and several passengers wounded for refusing to help unloading.

4 August 1981 Name unknown. Off town of Buenavista, Samar island, Philippines. A ferry was attacked by 50 guerillas of the Communist New People's Army who killed five and wounded four.

31 August 1981 *Nuria 767.* 17 miles off Cagayan de Tawitawi island, 500 miles south of Manila, *en route* for Sabah. A 135-ton motor launch. Two stowaway pirates and two crew members looted vessel, and lined up and shot 11 people. 48 others jumped overboard and 25 were drowned. Pirates took $380,000 in cash and $126,000 in kind.

September 1981 Name unknown. 66 kilometres off Sandakan. A cargo ship was fired at with a machine gun but refused to stop, and escaped.

September 1981 *Kimanis.* Singapore registry. 3079-ton passenger/general cargo ferry. Near Kalimantan. Pirates opened fire from speedboats but ship did not stop.

7 October 1981 Name unknown. Off Semporna. Five armed men who were holding the ship were surprised by police who shot two of them.

---

15 January 1982 *Hegg.* Japanese registry. 9034 tons. About 21 miles east of Mindanao. Fired on by two Philippine Air Force aircraft as they were 'suspected of carrying terrorists and some ten million dollars worth of arms and explosives'.

24 January 1982 *Ikan Mas.* Off Natunas Islands. A Malaysian fishing boat off the Natunas Islands 80 miles north-east of Singapore. At first the pirate boat was thought to be police boat but later identified as flying the skull and cross-bones flag. Eight pirates armed with sub-machine guns stole cash, valuables, and fish worth $40,000. Malaysian police warn that the Natunas are known to be a hideout for pirates.

5 February 1982 *World Unicorn*. British registry. 256,652-ton tanker. Off Jakarta. The officers were held at knife-point and the ship's safe robbed by two Indonesians.

27 March 1982 *Afran Star*. Liberian registry. Tanker. Makassar Strait off Borneo. No details available.

9 March 1982 *Josephine*. Senipah, Borneo. Pirate attack repelled. No details available.

May 1982 *Voyager*. 45-foot yacht. Manila Bay. Approaching Manila from Hong Kong at 0145 when five pirates armed with guns and long knives boarded from small motorised boat. Stole about £30,000 and much equipment.

26 December 1982 *Santa Lucia*. Pagadian. A ferry damaged by a bomb explosion killing two and injuring 50. Believed to be the target of the Moro National Liberation Front.

February 1983 *Juncta Maru*. Musi River, Indonesia. Cash and valuables stolen and some arrests made.

April 1983 *Quedlingburg*. East German ship. *En route* from Singapore to Surabaya. Unsuccessful pirate attack. No details available.

10 April 1983 *Sidharta*. Yacht. Off Spratly Islands. Shelled and set on fire. One crew member killed. Believed to have been done by Vietnamese soldiers.

17 October 1983 Name unknown. 44 kilometres off Sandakan. Five fishermen reported missing after being shot at from two speedboats.

23 October 1983 *Sara Hashim*. Off Spratly Island. No details available.

February 1984 *Vietnamese*. Palawan Islands. Three Vietnamese refugee girls found after being raped by fishermen and abandoned on remote island.

17 February 1984 Name unknown. Off Pulau Mataking, near Sabah. One fisherman killed and two wounded when fired on.

11 August 1984 Name unknown. Near Bulu Bulu Island in the Tawi group. A small passenger vessel attacked by three men armed with sub-machine guns. 33 people killed, more wounded, and three young girls abducted. 200,000 pesos stolen.

Reports of Piracy in the Central and South America Area

The incidents concerning small craft which are believed to have been due to the drug smuggling trade are included in the section on piracy of small craft and yachts.

27 December 1980 *Schwabenstein*. West German registry. 16,199 tons. Buenaventura, Colombia.

20 March 1981 *Mar Negro*. Spanish registry. 14,620-ton general cargo ship. Buenaventura, Colombia. During the stay in port the ship was robbed on several occasions, both cargo and cabins, despite police being on board. On leaving harbour, she was boarded at 0215 by seven armed men from a fast launch while in the buoyed channel. These fired several shots to intimidate the crew who locked themselves in to the 'citadel'. Thieves broke open a container and lowered 160 hair-dryers into their launch before leaving the ship at 0235.

• Map p86–7

22 June 1981 *Unterturkheim*. West German registry. 15,767 tons. Barranquilla, Colombia.

November 1981 *Banbury*. British registry. 15,749 tons. Santos.

November 1981 *British Spey*. British registry. 25,590-ton tanker. Santos.

December 1981 *Kubbar*. South Korean registry. Buenaventura, Colombia.

31 January 1982 *Alta*. Liberian registry. 9247-ton bulk carrier. Off Puerto Cabezas, Nicaragua. Approached by small motor boat from nearby cove at 1020 while stopped and repairing engines. Motor boat contained seven men, four of them dressed in guerilla uniforms. At 1115 the *Alta* was underway but the boat was within 300 yards of the ship's stern and pirates started firing and this continued for half an hour. Meanwhile the *Alta* manoeuvred and attempted to ram the pirates' boat which could not approach from astern because of the ship's propellors. The pirates eventually left at 1145 and had evidently come from another cargo ship anchored in the cove which they had probably taken over earlier. Some 50 bullet holes discovered subsequently and a number of window safety-glasses broken, evidently by bullets.

12 April 1982 *Joseph Lykes*. US registry. 14,515-ton general cargo ship. Guayaquil, Ecuador. Boarded by pirates and cargo robbed. No details available.

13 April 1982 *James Lykes.* US registry. 14,515-ton general cargo ship. Cartagena, Colombia. Boarded by pirates and cargo robbed. No details available.

June 1982 *Costa Andaluza.* Spanish registry. 500 tons. Cabo San Lorenzo, Colombia.

June 1982 *Nordbay.* Singapore registry. Kingston, Jamaica.

5 June 1982 *British Kennet.* British registry. 25,531-ton tanker. Santos, Brazil alongside Alemoa jetty. Ship boarded from a rowing boat while alongside at 2340. Master discovered thieves on entering his ransacked cabin. He was immediately struck on the head, knocked down, and kicked in the ribs. Then he was bound and gagged while a knife was held in his face. He was dragged into his bedroom but remembers little else until the thieves left in a hurry, and he was able to escape from his bonds. Alarm raised by chief officer who saw thief carrying two suitcases past his cabin. Thieves threw gear over the side into their rowing boat and left. Ship's lifeboat was lowered to give chase but did not succeed in catching them. Police were informed but no assistance materialised.

11 November 1982 *Orient Coral.* Liberan registry. 46,545-ton bulk carrier. Santos.

3 February 1983 *Golden Wave.* Santos, Brazil. Master's cabin was forced open while he was ashore and money and personal effects stolen.

12 March 1983 *Amelia Topic.* Liberian registry. 62,355-ton bulk carrier. Santos, Brazil. Ship's safe removed bodily and some personal effects stolen while the master was ashore.

21 March 1983 *Strider Crystal.* Santos, Brazil. The safe was taken away bodily together with the master's personal belongings while he was ashore.

20 April 1983 *Lips.* Greek registry. 15,059 tons. Santos, Brazil. The safe was taken away together with some personal belongings while the master was ashore.

3 June 1983 *Benvorlich.* British registry. 38,711-ton bulk carrier. Santos, Brazil. Discharging cargo at private terminal up a creek beyond the main port. Master was woken at 0150 by door being forced open by jemmies and a man with a revolver appeared. One other man with a knife joined the intruder while a third remained outside in the day cabin. The master tried to make a noise to alert the nearby radio officer but was struck on the head with the revolver, dragged through to his day room, and made to lie spread-eagled face down on the deck. Intruders found the safe and asked master for keys by putting a loaded and cocked revolver in his mouth; stole £2300. The master was tied face down on his bunk and gagged. Intruders enjoyed his drink and left less than fifteen minutes after they had arrived, and the master managed to raise alarm. Subsequently he was informed that there was an average of one major shipboard robbery each night, though more usually in the main port or the waiting anchorage outside. He gave an interview to a television company who run a programme on shipboard robberies in Santos at peak viewing time each Saturday night.

20 June 1983 *Yaguari*. Santos, Brazil. The seals of two containers were broken and part of the contents pilfered. Two of the thieves tried to attack the officer on duty and ran away down the gangway to a small boat which drew away quickly.

25 June 1983 *Takachiho Maru*. Japanese registry(?) Santos, Brazil. Boarded by six thieves. Master tried to stop them and had his forehead injured and hands tied after which the thieves searched his cabin and forced him to open the safe.

8 July 1983 *Neptune C.* Greek registry. 68,401-ton bulk carrier. Santos, Brazil. The ship's safe was forced open while the master was ashore.

21 July 1983 *Asia Honesty*. Liberian registry. 25,320-ton bulk carrier. Santos, Brazil. Thieves climbed the ship's side from a launch and stole many items from a crew member's cabin.

2 August 1983 *Margas*. Santos, Brazil. No details available.

19 August 1983 *Great Universe*. 16,438 tons. Santos, Brazil. Armed thieves broke into the master's cabin and stole money and personal effects.

9 September 1983 *Angelic Protector*. Greek registry. 77,961-ton bulk carrier. Santos, Brazil, berthed alongside and discharging potash cargo. Chief officer heard noise from his cabin at 2030 and went to investigate. Two men, wearing stocking masks, put guns at his head and back, tied him up, and carried him into the captain's cabin which had been ransacked. One or two more thieves were there and one was trying to open the safe with a hammer and iron lever. When he did not succeed, the safe was removed bodily. The thieves also took the chief officer's ring from his hand. They were seen leaving in a speedboat. After ten minutes, the chief officer released himself and called police who arrived at 2115.

September 1983 *Almaloz.* Santos, Brazil. No details available

September 1983 *Yaguan.* Santos, Brazil. No details available.

September 1983 Master of *Durian* advised by charterer's representative that many ships alongside in Santos have had armed burglars attack the master's cabin to steal the safe or its contents. In several cases where the captain has tried to resist, he has been tortured and forced to hand over the safe key and, in a few cases, shot at.

7 September 1983 *Durian.* Santos, Brazil. Advised by representative from charterers that many ships alongside in Santos have had armed burglars attempt to steal the safe and contents from master's cabin. In several cases where the master has tried to resist, or to refuse to hand over the key, he has been tortured and forced to do so and also, in a few cases, shot at. Thieves boarded during the night and broke their way into the lounge and the master's cabin. They removed the ship's safe, containing $2,720, drugs, and some private foreign currency and a gold wrist-watch. Burglary discovered at 0600 and port police informed. Master states 'I claim that Santos is the only major port in the world where authorities are aware that foreign captains are regularly robbed, hurt and humiliated by organized men, while ships are alongside in a well guarded and organized port ...'

13 September 1983 *Kapetanissa.* Greek registry. 54,540 ton bulk carrier. Santos. Brazil. Loss of $3,000 and some personal items reported. Some crew members seriously wounded. No other details available.

20 September 1983 Article in *O Estado de Sao Paulo* summarising 22 robberies which have taken place within the port of Santos in the past eight months and also stating that the International Shipping Federation have classified Santos as a dangerous port.

1 December 1983 Report in Lloyds List that between 50 and 100 armed robberies had occurred on ships in Santos.

1 December 1983 Names unknown. Santos. Reported that 50 to 100 vessels had been attacked during the past two years, usually by three to five men with help from the night gang of stevedores.

25 December 1983 *Lago Izabal.* Tampico, Mexico. Guatemalan ship. No details available.

February 1984 *Oroya* Santos, Brazil. Advised by agent on arrival that, towards the end of 1983, two ships had been boarded by Pirates armed with machine guns, the crews rounded up, and most of their belongings stolen.

Piracy of Small Craft and Yachts World-wide

1979 Thailand. 40-ton yacht challenged off Nakhon Si Thamarrat coast, Thailand. Two men switched on spreader lights and sat on deck, allowing light to reflect off their two M16 rifle barrels. They had no further trouble.

10 February 1979 Yacht *L'Artemis de Pytheas.* Six days out of Cebu in the Philippines *en route* for Brunei. Small boat overtook rapidly from astern and came alongside. Mrs Tangvald opened fire and was immediately shot in the head and killed. Owner, Peter Tangvald, with young 2¾-year-old son clinging to him, were spared. Pirate boat sheered off and disappeared after taking money and gun.

June 1979 Yacht *Kim.* Gulf of Thailand. Off Nakorn Si Thammarat and advised by police to go to a safer area as there were many pirates whom they could not control. Headed south for Songkla. Woken at 0200 by large grey boat close alongside with two spotlights on them. Two armed men with rifles standing ready to board and half a dozen others ready on the foredeck. Yacht opened fire with AK47 rifle and killed two men with guns and sprayed remainder. Attackers sheered off. One wounded pirate rescued from sea and he stated that attackers were part of a protection racket dealing with fishing boats in that area.

1980 Yacht *L'Artemis de Pytheas.* Gabes, Tunisia. Attacked while at anchor by three robbers armed with knives and clubs. Owner and woman beaten up and attempted rape of woman. Money taken. The gang were traced through the rather special radio which they stole.

Early 1980 Yacht *Gapa*. Vigie Cove, Castries, St Lucia. Boarded by three drug running bandits. One bandit shot, one drowned, and one arrested.

April 1980 Yacht *Kalia III*. Norman Cay, Bahamas. Yacht discovered with blood everywhere, owner dead in the dinghy which was riddled with bullet holes, and gun and cash missing. It is thought that the yacht stumbled on to a drug exchange and the occupants were killed by smugglers.

1981 *Explorer II*. Off Colombia. A shrimp boat was reported seized by drug smugglers.

1981 Yacht *Star III*. Off Riohacha, Colombia. A fishing boat reported attacked by pirates.

17 March 1981 Yacht *Sabie Star*. Anchored at Belem, Paraguay. Three armed robbers in a canoe stole clothes and cameras and passports and cut the yacht adrift. One robber was caught later and some items were recovered. The leader of the gang was rumoured to be a wanted murderer.

11 July 1981 Yacht *Cheers*. Friendship Bay, Bequia in the Windward Islands. Jim Holman and Betsy Hitz were attacked by a naked Bequian armed with a machete. Jim Holman was stabbed in the chest and stomach and attempts made at rape. All money stolen.

27 July 1981 Yacht *Saint Peter*. Barranquilla, Colombia. Hijacked by a group of narcotics traffickers while berthed.

September 1981 Yacht *Edna Maree*. Off Pulo Lankani. Pirates in Thai fishing boat swarmed on board. The Australian skipper, James Montgomery, threw the first in the water and pushed the second back into the fishing boat. The third stabbed him in the stomach and nearly cut off his right hand. Three pirates raped one woman; a second woman and child escaped by hiding below decks.

4 September 1981 Yacht *Susan Ann II*. Hijacked by three armed men who took the vessel to Cartagena, Colombia where they were captured by local authorities. Probably local narcotics traffickers. Report not confirmed.

October 1981 Yacht *Apsaru*. Anchored in the Maldives. Boarded by 'officials' accompanied by some fishermen. The crew were seized and tied up, robbed of money and cameras. Although jailed and fined $1,000 the attackers finally escaped.

December 1981 Three sailing boats attacked off Bahamas and robbed of cash and supplies.

November 1981 to May 1983
Yacht name unknown. Tobago. Yachtsman strangled whilst on board at anchor.

Yacht name unknown. Grenada. Shots exchanged between crew of Swedish yacht and an off-duty policeman. The crew were detained for a couple of days and then released. One Grenadian crew member drowned after a gunshot wound.

Yacht name unknown. Castries Harbour, St Lucia. American couple on board at anchor were robbed at gunpoint and woman raped.

Early 1982 Names Unknown. Turks and Caicos Islands. Some yachts were fired on near sunken wrecks.

Early 1982 Yacht *Nyn*. Near Port of Spain, Trinidad. Michael Crocker strangled on board by armed intruder.

Early 1982 Yacht *Belle Esprit*. Off Nassau. Attacked by five speedboats but rescued by police spotter plane. Reported fifty bullet holes in the hull.

24 January 1982 Malaysian fishing boat *Ikan Mas*. Off Natunas Islands in South China Sea. Pirate boat was at first thought to be a Malaysian police boat but was then seen to be flying the skull and cross-bones. Eight pirates armed with sub-machine guns stole cash, valuables, and fish worth $40,000. Malaysian police warn that Natunas are known to be a hideout for pirates.

May 1982 Yacht *Voyager*. Manila Bay. 45 foot. Approaching Manila from Hong Kong at 0145 when five pirates armed with guns and long knives boarded from small motorised boat. Stole about £30,000 and much equipment.

January 1983 Yacht *Renica*. Antigua. Attacked and robbed.

22 February 1983 Names unknown. Gulf of Fonseca. Two Nicaraguan fishing vessels attacked by El Salvoradean armed launches.

10 April 1983 Yacht *Sidharta*. Off Spratly Islands. Shelled and set on fire. One crew member killed. This may have been caused by Vietnamese soldiers.

June 1983 Yacht *Lucy of Wessex*. Antigua. Robbed while at anchor.

17 October 1983 Name unknown. 44 kilometres off Sandakan, off east coast of Sabah in the Sulu Sea. Five fishermen reported missing after being shot at from two speedboats.

February 1984 Yacht *Severance*. Deep Bay, Antigua. Attacked at night when at anchor by two black men who appeared to be full of alcohol and drugs. All crew were tied up and the yacht taken out to sea where one woman was raped by both black men. They brought the yacht back to Antigua where the owners succeeded in overpowering one black man while the other had gone ashore. The police were called and one man arrested. The second man was arrested later but is reported to have escaped subsequently.

17 February 1984 Fishing boat name unknown. Off Pulau Mataking near Sabah. One fisherman killed and two wounded when fired on.

No date Yacht name unknown. Exumas Islands. William and Pat Kemerara murdered when their yacht apparently stumbled across a drug transfer to Exumas Islands.

No date Yacht *Polymer III*. Between Bimini and Florida coast. Walter Falconer, his companion and the yacht disappeared without trace. Reasons unknown.

No date Yacht *Snowbound*. Near Williams Island, Bahamas. Peter Beamborough and Michael Collesta attacked and shot-up but escaped.

No date Name unknown. 10 miles south of Santa Marta, Colombia. All on board killed.

No date Name unknown. Belem, Brazil. Yacht robbed by thieves who woke nobody but cleared the boat.

No date Name unknown. Anchored south of Borneo. Owner surprised in the night by men armed with knives who cleared the boat, including the sails and even unbolted and removed the engine.

No date Name unknown. Anchored off West Africa. Boarded at night by two intruders. The owner wakened by noise as one thief tripped over and he shot and killed both with his revolver. He decided that the authorities might not approve so departed.

No date *Sea Wind.* Palmyra Island, Pacific. Yacht found in atoll with no sign of owner or wife. Wife's skull subsequently found and the culprits were brought to justice.

Reports of Terrorist and similar types of Attack World-wide

December 1979 *Ibsa Uno* and *Ibsa Tres.* Corcubion Bay, near Corunna, Spain. Attacked by magnetic mines with negligible damage.

11 January 1980 *General R Gumuspala.* Turkish general cargo vessel. 24 miles west of Beirut. Intercepted by corvettes and fired at with machine guns.

• Map p88–9

2 April 1980 *Ibsa Uno* and *Ibsa Dos.* Spanish whaler, Marin, Spain. Sunk by magnetic mines and refloated on 3 June and 14 June respectively.

22 May 1980 *Garmomar.* Spanish trawler. Off coast of Western Sahara near Dakhla. Seized by Polisario guerillas and grounded. Total loss.

4 June 1980 *Rio Vouga.* Portuguese trawler. Off Western coast of Sahara. Boarded by Polisario guerillas who kidnapped the crew.

2 July 1980 *Cap Juby II.* Moroccan trawler. Off Morocco. Bombarded and attacked by Polisario guerillas. Abandoned and total loss.

2 July 1980 *Moroboro.* Cuban supply and transport vessel. 30 miles off Villa Cisneros, Western Sahara. Fired on by unidentified war planes killing the master and seriously wounding two other officers.

7 July 1980 *Khalil.* Lebanese general cargo ship. Aquamarina, Lebanon. Attacked by Phalangists and set on fire. Towed out, dynamited, and sunk in Jounieh Bay.

12 July 1980 *Gilberta Pico.* Cuban supply and transport vessel. 30 miles off Villa Cisneros, Western Sahara. Fired on by unidentified war planes, injuring the first officer.

29 September 1980 *Sarita.* Spanish fishing vessel. North of Dakhla, Western Sahara. Boarded by Polisario guerillas who kidnapped the crew.

29 September 1980 *Costa de Terranova.* Spanish trawler.

North of Dakhla, Western Sahara. Boarded by Polisario guerillas who kidnapped the crew.

2 October 1980 *Denebe*. Portuguese trawler. Off Western coast of Sahara. Seized by Polisario guerillas who kidnapped the crew.

29 October 1980 *Dat Assawari*. Libyan frigate. Genoa. A bomb explosion blew a three metre hole above the water line while the ship was undergoing a refit. Believed to be the work of the Maltese Nationalist front.

14 November 1980 *Ampere*. French cable laying vessel. One kilometre off coast near Beirut. Fired on by unidentified gunmen while repairing a telephone cable.

6 February 1981 *Nellie M*. British general cargo ship. Sunk in Lough Foyle off Moville by an Irish Republican Army (IRA) explosion.

27 February 1981 *Rached*. Lebanese general cargo ship. Tyre, Lebanon. Damaged by explosion on board causing flooding. Vessel grounded and sank.

16 April 1981 *Manal S*. Lebanese general cargo ship Sidon, Lebanon. Dynamited, probably by Israeli frogmen, resulting in flooding of the engine room and serious damage to the starboard side. Grounded.

22 May 1981 *Rola Rana*. Lebanese general cargo ship. Sidon, Lebanon. Sank after plastic charge exploded. Probably caused by Israeli frogmen.

7 June 1981 *Iliana Bay*. Cotabato City, Philippines. Hijacked by either local terrorists or pirates who forced the ship to proceed to another destination to unload its cargo of rice. The master was reportedly stabbed to death and several passengers wounded for refusing to help with the unloading.

22 July 1981 *Saint Peter*. Colombian general cargo ship. Bárranquilla, Colombia. Stolen by a group of narcotics traffickers while berthed.

4 August 1981 Name unknown. Ferry. Off Buenavista Town, Samar Island, Philippines. Attacked by 50 guerillas of the Communist New People's Army killing five and wounding four.

22 August 1981 *Hai Feng*. Chinese general cargo ship. Beirut. A shell fell on the edge of the quay alongside the vessel causing a large hole below the waterline.

26 September 1981 *Porto Ceu.* Portuguese fishing vessel. Off Western Sahara coast. Attacked by guerillas of the Polisario Front who killed one fisherman and wounded three others.

2 October 1981 *Marques de la Ensenada.* Spanish destroyer. Santander. Basque guerillas exploded device which caused severe damage.

2 January 1982 *Babanaft One.* Panamian tanker. Tripoli, Lebanon. Shelled and set on fire.

15 January 1982 *Hegg.* Japanese oil/chemical tanker. 21 miles east of Mindanao, Philippines. Fired on by two Philippine Air Force aircraft as 'suspected of carrying terrorists and some $10 million worth of arms and explosives.'

31 January 1982 *Alta.* Liberian bulk carrier. Off Puerto Cabezas, Nicaragua. Approached by small motor boat from nearby cove at 1020 while stopped and repairing engines. Motor boat contained seven men, four of them dressed in guerilla uniforms. At 1115 the *Alta* was underway but the boat was within 300 yards of the ship's stern and pirates started firing and this continued for half an hour. Meanwhile the *Alta* manoeuvred and attempted to ram the pirate's boat which could not approach from astern because of the ship's propellors. Eventually the pirates left at 1145 and had evidently come from another cargo ship anchored in the cove which they had probably taken over earlier. Some 50 bullet holes discovered subsequently and a number of window safety glasses broken, evidently by bullets.

23 February 1982 *Saint Bedan.* British general cargo ship. Lough Foyle. Sank after IRA placed explosive device on board.

9 March 1982 *Rached.* Lebanese general cargo ship. Tyre. Believed dynamited by Israeli frogmen, causing vessel to ground.

27 July 1982 *Flora.* West German Red Cross relief vessel. Jounieh, Lebanon. Struck by rocket, killing one crew member.

15 September 1982 *Nash 5.* British non-propelled bucket dredger. Beirut. Sank after being struck by a projectile. Refloated and towed to Piraeus for repairs.

26 December 1982 *Santa Lucia.* Philippine ferry. Pagadian. Damaged by bomb placed by Moro National Liberation Front. 2 killed and 50 injured.

22 February 1983 Names unknown. Gulf of Fonseca. Two Nicaraguan fishing vessels attacked by El Salvadorean armed launches.

28–30 March 1983 *Ho Ming No 7*. Puerto Saudino, Nicaragua. Attacked by two Piranha submersible craft while loading sugar. No details available.

17 April 1983 Two Portuguese trawlers. Off Western Sahara. Machine gunned by gunboats manned by Polisario guerillas.

Miscellaneous Reports of Attacks not Covered Elsewhere

February 1979 *Alysse Maru*. US Naval Research ship (converted minesweeper 320 tons). Maldive Islands. Put into port for engine repairs. 300 islanders in dug-out canoes, armed with machetes, spears, knives and small arms, came alongside and, after an exchange of gunfire, they overran the ship. Captain was led off ship with a noose about his neck when he and two others volunteered to leave in return for promise of safety for the remaining nine crew members. However they managed to send a message through a radio ham in Nairobi and US authorities are understood to have interceded through Maldivian Government.

22 February 1984 *Chevron Pacific*. Anchored in Visakhapatnam Roads on east Indian coast. On arrival and during anchoring at about 1900, four attempts were made by small wooden vessels to board using three or four grappling lines. First attempt was made while ship was still doing 14 knots and this and the second attempt failed. The other two attempts were repulsed by using water jets from foam monitors on deck.

18 February 1984 *Chevron Pacific*. Anchored in Madras Roads. At about 1000 the ship was boarded from a small sailing craft. Robbers cut off five 2.5in fire hose nozzles, and escaped before they could be caught.

26 February 1984 *Inverlock*. Liberian registry. 69,000-ton bulk carrier. Barcelona, Spain. Vessel at coal berth discharging. At 0300 master was woken in bed by someone threatening him with a knife and saw two thieves – one black and one white. They forced him to open the safe and stole $1,200 and then stole his personal cash and wrist-watch. Then they left him tied and gagged on his bed.

Appendix

Anti-Piracy Measures
PROPOSED MEASURES ON BOARD SHIP

This information has been collated by the International Maritime Bureau (IMB) and International Maritime Organisation (IMO)

The Baltic and International Maritime Conference have also released details of measures adopted by their members in dealing with the threat of piracy in West Africa. The precautions are as follows:

1. Cargo lights overside

2. A minimum of two watchmen must be used to patrol decks continuously in addition to the duty officer. On approach of pirate boats, sound the whistle in a series of rapid blasts. Safety helmets should be provided and heavy clothing worn to lessen the impact of broken glass and explosive blast. A good supply of missiles should be ready on board. These can be effectively made from empty beer bottles filled with sand. Empty beer bottles are not recommended since many of them do not break and merely can be thrown back. Hoses should be rigged on both sides of the vessel, at least three on each side. The fire pump should be started and water pressure on deck should be maintained throughout the hours of darkness with the hoses running. The hoses can be loosely lashed to the bulwarks.

3. If the vessel is fitted with a searchlight this should be used to scan the surrounding waters. The Aldis lamp can be used to the same effect.

4. Walkie-talkies or vessel's loud hailer system should be in operation for direct communication between the watchmen and duty officer.

5. Anchor hawsepipes should be closed with plates provided.

6. For additional protection, weld main storeroom doors using a short length of pipe. This pipe can be tack welded on to the bulwark and door edge. This has proved to be far more effective than padlocks.

Emergency Drill in case of Pirates Boarding
1. If it proves impossible to stop pirates boarding then all crew members should come inside the accommodation.

2. There should be only one entrance remaining open, all others to be securely battened down. This entrance must then be secured.

3. The continuous ringing of the general alarm bell is the signal for everyone to go down into the engine room, as quickly as possible. Again only one entrance to remain open.

4. One man to be detailed to check that everybody is inside and to then secure the last remaining door. This means that everybody is enclosed in the steel engine compartment. Generators could be stopped in order to black out the vessel depending on the circumstances and bearing in mind that there would be no ventilation in the engine room itself.

As a general recommendation, vessels should steam out to sea during the evening and lie fifteen miles off the general anchor position, since from this distance VHF contact is still possible at Lagos and Port Harcourt.

Use of Stronger Deterrents
1. Guns – here one must remember that the prime object is to repel and frighten off boarders, not to kill them. In cases where pirates are unarmed, a shot-gun fired in the air from the main deck would be an extremely effective deterrent. In cases where

pirates are armed, there is no other choice but to retreat to the most safe place on board, for instance, the engine room. During the first attack when the pirates were caught red-handed by police, they immediately tried to implicate the vessel by false allegations. This involved certain crew members who were supposedly bribed to allow them on board.

2. Gas bombs - tear gas would be extremely effective against pirate boats. Even in strong winds, the short duration of concentrated gas would cause chaos and provide a useful deterrent against boarders.

INTERNATIONAL SHIPPING FEDERATION

The International Shipping Federation have issued the following consolidated list of preventative measures known to be adopted by some shipowning companies in countering armed attacks.

Preventative measures known to be adopted by some companies in combating armed robbery.

1. Rather than remaining in anchorages where ships are most vulnerable to attack, either:

steam at least 20 and up to 40 miles off shore at night and only returning within VHF range at regular intervals for orders/news from agents; or

drift (with the engines on stand-by) out of sight of the coast/port (about 40–50 miles offshore) at night.

2. When it is necessary to anchor inshore; choose an anchorage away from the fairway, extinguishing all lighting and not reporting exact position by radio to signal station.

3. Strengthening night watches, with continuous patrols and forecastle head policing and walkie-talkie contact between watch-keepers and the bridge.

4. Maintaining constant short-range radar watch; broadcasting on VHF the presence of suspicious craft, seen either visually or on radar; sounding a general alarm by ship's whistle to alert the crew and other vessels.

5. Sealing off all possible means of access to the ship, eg fitting hawsepipe plates; locking doors and hatch covers; removing all ladders/gangways; maintaining a constant supply of water to the hawsepipes.

6. Lighting fully the deck, sides and bow and having searchlights and Aldis lamp ready for use. Equipping bridge wings with searchlights.

7. Sealing off securely access to the accommodation spaces.

8. Rigging fire and deck wash-hose with water pressure on.

9. Removing all portable equipment from the deck.

10. Stowing containers loaded with valuables door to door and in tiers.

11. Cruising while awaiting pilot.

12. Issuing minimum number of cargo manifests, with only a general description of the cargo if possible.

13. Increasing speed to seaward when approached by small boats or boarded by pirates to prevent canoes following and to impede the transfer of stolen goods into craft alongside.

To date, it has been recommended that firearms should *not* be issued to crew members.

COMMERCIAL MEASURES

During the course of the past year, a number of private security organisations have proposed programmes available to shipowners to assist in the protection of their vessels.

Piracy Today

One such programme has as its objectives, the following:

1. The avoidance of piracy by advance intelligence, anticipation and evasive action.

2. Deterring pirates by the state of preparedness of the vessel.

3. Deterring pirates in the process of boarding the vessel.

4. The creation of an environment which will disorientate and confuse pirates who have managed to board the vessel and at the same time give the crew members sufficient time to seek protection and safety on the vessel.

5. Minimisation of loss and damage to the vessel and its cargo.

6. The alerting of the local security authorities and agencies and nearby vessels thus increasing the chances of obtaining assistance.

The programme is based largely on the training of crews and the provision and installation of special equipment. The range of equipment proposed is of particular interest, and includes:

1. Military style trip-wire system modified to maritime requirements, secured with 'G' clamp type brackets, which activates a flare when triggered.

2. Electrically detonated stun packages (several times more powerful than standard military issue) specially developed for maritime use in water-tight housing.

3. Standard military stun package discharged with special pistol to a range of approximately 80 metres.

4. Retrievable barbed tape secured to removable brackets round the side of a vessel.

5. Halon fire extinguisher weighing a few ounces and carried in a purpose made webbing holster, for optional use against pirates at close quarters.

6. Remote detection and signalling system using fibre optics which detects pirates attempting to board a vessel and alerts an audible/visible annunciator located on the bridge.

7. Still not fully developed or tested is a system of trailing fibres designed to snarl the propellor of small craft in close proximity to the stern of a vessel.

Shipowners may feel the adoption of such measures to be worthwhile, particularly in known high-risk areas. The existence of such programmes should not, however, be seen as an alternative to the need for effective governmental action to eradicate armed attacks on shipping.

RECOMMENDED PRECAUTIONS FOR YACHTSMEN ISSUED BY US COAST GUARD

Since many long-range cruising yachtsmen follow relaxed, flexible schedules, hijackers have time to make their runs and dispose of owners, crew and vessel before friends or relatives of the victims are aware that something is wrong.

As a yachtsman there are several measures you can take to protect your vessel and its party. For one - know your crew. Particularly, hired crewmen. But do not overlook that last minute guest who decided to come along for the ride. Insist on positive identification of anyone not an established friend. Do this no matter how short your intended trip. As silly as it sounds - ask to see a social security card and a second ID with a photograph or physical description. If they're not a citizen, ask for a passport, entry visa or alien registration. But don't stop at just seeing the information. Record the person's name, date and place of birth and any official numbers on the document. Before you leave, personally deliver or mail a complete crew and passenger list to someone you trust along with a float plan and instructions to notify the coast guard if you fail to arrive at your destination within a reasonable length of time. Let everyone aboard know that this has been done and do not fail to update the list if additional crew or passengers are picked up along the way.

Always check your boat for stowaways - just before you leave.

If, during your voyage, you go to the assistance of anyone found in apparent distress - make every effort to contact the nearest coast guard radio facility or any coastal radio station and describe the situation and your intentions before you go. Be alert to any unusual occurrence which doesn't seem to fit the normal pattern and be especially wary when the distressed person(s) insist on boarding your vessel (unless his has sunk).

When departing on a foreign cruise from a US port, consider taking the time to clear with the local customs agent. Although this is not required for pleasure boats, it could be time well spent. Give the agent a complete crew list and on customs form No 4455, list all firearms, high value personal property and portable boat equipment. Record foreign made cameras, optical and navigation equipment, etc and list serial numbers or carbide engraved identification numbers. Retain a certified copy. This provides you a record which may be valuable in cases of loss for whatever cause, and could save you considerable time and trouble entering and clearing foreign ports or when returning to the US.

Another good idea is to travel with another yacht. Groups of two or three boats travelling together are far less likely candidates for trouble than a single boat. It is also prudent when anchored at night to keep a live watch on deck.

The use of firearms aboard a yacht for protection is a highly debatable issue from the coast guard's viewpoint. There is no prohibition against carrying firearms for this purpose so long as they are not defined as illegal under the Firearms Act – for instance, sawed-off shotguns or automatic weapons. You might want to consider though, that your own weapons mightly easily be used against you by hijackers, and, at best, could provoke a troublesome experience with suspicious foreign police or port officials.

Travel in pairs when possible.

Above all – don't over react. Remember, only a relatively few yachts are actually hijacked. If you plan ahead, follow the guidelines and don't get careless, your boating experiences can continue to be the pleasure they have been in the past.

If you think your boat has been stolen we'll do our best to help you find it, but remember, your best protection against hijacking is to follow the preventive measures stated earlier:

- Know your crew – check ID's, make a list, update it, give it to a trusted friend before you leave.

- File a float plan – then follow it.

- Check for stowaways.

- Be alert for unusual situations.

- If possible, contact the coast guard before giving assistance to another vessel.

- Clear with the local customs agent – it can't hurt and it may help.

Index of Ship Names